Thousand Dollar Hour:

Funding College Through Scholarships

By Hannah Rivard

ISBN-10: 1484134028

ISBN-13: 978-1484134023

You're applying for scholarships at your own risk. I take no liability for brain damage, paper cuts, sleepless nights, or failure to fund college through scholarships. Similarly, if you fund all of college through scholarships, that's awesome, and you can take the credit.

Because your success is up to you.

thou$and dollar h☉ur™ dollar

Better one handful with tranquility than two handfuls with toil and
chasing after the wind.

~Ecclesiastes 4:6 (NIV)

Table of Contents

INTRODUCTION

This book, *Thousand Dollar Hour: Funding College Through Scholarships,* is packed with every tip I learned in my years of successful scholarship hunting, including the following:

1. The number one place you should be looking for scholarships—but never do.

2. How to double your money on select scholarships with a single mouse click.

3. The way to exponentially increase your chances of getting a scholarship simply through the process of elimination.

4. The one aspect of the scholarship timeline few people mention but can earn you scholarships no one else thinks to look for.

5. The one scholarship search engine everyone uses obsessively but you should barely use at all.

6. How to identify the scholarships you'll probably never get so you can invest your time on those you might.

7. A database of over 20 scholarship search engines, and my reviews of which are the best and which are the worst.

I've made every attempt to make this book as friendly and interesting as possible, and sometimes my writing is a little informal. (I may have even ended a sentence with a preposition once or twice.) But in the end, I think it made for a less painful book, because, after all, there are more interesting topics out there than scholarships. Yet at the same time, there is little that should be more interesting to college students than scholarships, because winning them will likely be the best paying job they'll ever have!

Happy reading!

Hannah Rivard

June 2012

CHAPTER 1:

My Story

"There are millions of dollars of unclaimed scholarships out there."

I stared at my glittering computer screen. "Where?" I groaned. I had heard that said a million times, and here it was on yet another college website. But I had combed FastWeb and Scholarships.com and a dozen other sites, and every scholarship seemed to have two hundred other students competing for it. If there were "unclaimed scholarships," they didn't exist in my universe.

However, I didn't worry about it much until my senior year of high school in 2009. I sat on my faded blue couch, looking at the letter in my hands. A full ride. In the pages, it showed glossy photos of smiling students and outlined the college's offer: books, room and board, tuition, and even flights home. Yet I turned it down; some things in life are more important than saving money. I knew that was not the school I needed to go to for the best education for my mind and soul, and I was entirely confident I was to go to Northwestern College in St. Paul, Minnesota.

However, the highest scholarship Northwestern offered was half tuition. So, I bit my lip, took a deep breath, and decided that if I couldn't get a full ride from the college, I would create my own full ride. Or, in other words, I determined that I would pay for school through scholarships.

Northwestern was going to cost upwards of $100,000, and I was determined that paying for my college education would not be a burden on my parents. Even more, I did not want to be strangled with tens of thousands of dollars of debt after I graduated, right at the moment in life when I should be most free to pursue the dreams God had given me and experience the life that awaited.

So spring 2009, the second semester of my senior year of high school, I began the scholarship quest. Weekends, late nights, school breaks—I worked tirelessly to find, apply for, and win scholarships to pay for my education. I made mistakes that cost me thousands of dollars and learned strategies that gained me thousands more.

Some nights at midnight, scrolling through the Internet for yet another scholarship, I wanted to give up. But I kept pushing forward, knowing that it would only be through unswerving dedication I would succeed.

And I did. Spring 2012, I graduated summa cum laude from Northwestern College with a bachelor's degree in Entrepreneurial Business. Better yet, in those three years, by the time I graduated I had earned nearly $100,000—enough to cover all my school expenses—by working just a few hours per month. And I learned that scholarships would probably become the best paying job I would ever have.

CHAPTER 2:

Excuses, Excuses

Students have a little panic attack when I tell them they should apply for scholarships. Before I've even finished my sentence they've buried me under at least fourteen reasons why they couldn't possibly ever in their lifetime even dream of hoping to apply for a scholarship.

So what are the most common objections toward scholarships?

1. **"Applying for scholarships takes too much time! Hours and hours of my life gone *forever*!"**

I know you're practically in college, but let's go back to elementary school math for a second here. You don't have time for scholarships. Okay, I get that. You're busy. You're working 20 hours a week.

Wait a second. You're working 20 hours a week, for, what, $10 an hour, $15 or $20 at most? And then you lose part of that money to taxes (unlike most scholarship money, we'll cover the subject of taxes later). Think about this.

Let's say you're a really great applier-for-scholarships (because you've read this book and know all the secrets) and for every ten hours you spend on scholarships, you win a $1,000 scholarship. $1,000/10 hours= $100/hour. Nice. Really nice.

Or, you could gripe that scholarships take too much time because you work some super important job. So to make the same amount of money, that's $1,000/$10/hour= 100 hours.

10 hours. 100 hours. And who was complaining about not having enough time?

Remember, scholarships are not extracurricular, something you fit in on the side. They are a job, you commit to it like a job, and as I said before, it'll probably be the best paying job you'll ever have.

2. **"My geriatric three-legged cat has better grades than I do. I'll never get a scholarship."**

While many scholarships do consider grades, there are large numbers of scholarships that don't even give grades a sideways glance—these scholarships are all about your character, involvement in your community, or life goals, for example. There are even scholarships specifically for students with *low* grade point averages. Scholarships aren't for perfect people. They're for *real* people.

3. **"I promise, I *totally* looked for scholarships, like, *at least* once. There were none that applied to me."**

That's because you weren't looking in the right areas. Don't worry, you were probably looking where everyone told you to, but "everyone" may be making the same mistakes. You need to look in the right places, and that's remarkably easy to do. There are scholarships that specifically apply to you—I mean, come on, did you know there are scholarships for *tall* people? (Check out Tall Clubs International.) There *are* scholarships out there for you, and I'll show you how to find them!

4. **"I've applied for all kinds of scholarships, and I've never won even one. Scholarships are dumb."**

Yeah, scholarships are dumb if you apply for them in a thoughtless manner, which is basically equivalent to running down the sidewalk hollering that you need money. Not helpful. That's why you develop a strategy to winning scholarships, know where to look for them, figure out how to apply, customize your application such that it blows the socks of the scholarship providers, and become a lean, mean, scholarship-winning machine.

5. **"I am so totally overwhelmed. I have no idea where to start."**

Listen, you're going to college. You made it through high school and Algebra II and English comp and the ACT and all those other tests. Scholarships are way easier than all those classes (and besides, you're not getting graded on scholarships!), which means you are totally smart enough to get scholarships—you just need some guidance. That's why at the end of this book I've summarized the main points of every chapter, plus given you a checklist and a timeline so it's completely clear what you need to do. You can do this!

6. **"I hate applying for scholarships! I'm a terrible writer, and it nearly killed me just applying for college. Now I have to apply for scholarships?! Give me a break!"**

I understand applying for scholarships is right up there on the fun-ness level with cleaning up after the dog and banging your head against a wall. But, believe me: paying off $100,000 in school debt without a cent of that coming from your bank account? That's money you could use for other things. Like a place to live. A vehicle to drive. And something better to eat than Ramen noodles.

CHAPTER 3:

Why You Should Love Scholarships

College costs money.

If you want to go to college, that might be a problem for you. You have a few options for paying for it:

1. **Rob a bank.** I don't generally recommend this. Regardless of some slight accompanying ethical issues, if you were caught, you would be living in a jail. Not a dorm room.

2. **Win the lottery.** This is a really great option, but, sadly, the odds are not exactly in your favor. You might have better chances at robbing that bank and escaping the maximum-security prison they'll put you in.

3. **Find buried treasure**. This could be super fun, albeit time consuming. Check out some books on treasure hunting from the library to jump-start your treasure hunting skills.

Some of you may want something a little more reliable than the aforementioned options, so I have a few more choices for you:

1. **Go to a really inexpensive school**. There are many fabulous inexpensive schools out there, and I encourage you to look seriously at them.

However, they don't always offer the major you want, are in the location you want, or offer the opportunities you know are crucial to your education and your personal development.

2. **Go where you're offered a full ride or good scholarship package**. As I said in my story earlier, however, sometimes those full rides don't come from the school you truly feel you should attend. Also, if you're relying entirely on college-specific scholarships to fund your education, you may feel pressured to attend a school that will not truly complete you simply because it gave you the best scholarship package.

3. **Work your way through college**. I have known dozens of students who did just this, and do you know what I saw? Burned-out, bleary-eyed zombies who worked harder than I thought humanly possible and hated every minute of it. They worked three jobs, took a full load, got no sleep, and had no time to live, rest, enjoy school, or pursue their passions. School controlled them; they didn't control it. I don't want that to happen to you.

4. **Don't work through college and simply accumulate loans**. You could just forget about it and rack up the loans instead of killing yourself to get scholarships or hold down a job. The thing is, go back and read the first line of this page. What was it? *College costs money.* Well, the interest you're going to pay on your student loans for the next hundred and fifty years is going to turn that statement into *College costs so much money selling your soul isn't going to get you out of debt.* And that's more true than you may realize: really, if you're strangled by debt for the next ten or twenty or more years, you're not going to be free to pursue your passions, live your dreams, and be the person God created you to be. Don't do that to yourself. It's not worth it.

That was the process I went through when trying to decide how to pay for scholarships. And even if you have a lot of money, or your parents are willing to pay for your school—wouldn't you rather have no one pay anything? Wouldn't you rather take advantage of money already out there earmarked for your education?

Of course. That money is out there, you can get it, and it's called scholarships. You pay for college through scholarships, and you have no long working hours, no interest, and no extra job. You can work in sweats and a t-shirt. You have the school you want and the education you want, and you can live life like you always wanted to live it.

And that's worth something.

CHAPTER 4:

Attitudes for Success

Role Playing

What are you doing when you apply for a scholarship?

"I'm getting money," you answer.

Wrong.

You're inspiring someone else to give you money—to fund your life and your dreams.

How is that different? Well, the mindset you take toward scholarships will determine how you apply. Are you just sending some random essay off into cyberspace, or are you seeking to connect with a real human being who cares deeply about the education of youth today?

One of the best ways to understand this is to do a bit of role playing. Imagine, for a moment, you're going to host a scholarship. (Actually, you've probably done something similar—have you ever hosted any sort of contest or judged a class? It's not that different.)

Let's say you run a music business and you've decided to help students who, like you, were talented and wanted to study music but didn't have the finances to do so. You're willing to invest many hours of your time and thousands of your dollars into one or more students, so clearly education and social responsibility are important to you. You'd like to choose a student who reminds you of yourself—has had his or her life radically changed by the power of music and wants to share that with others.

You're a little concerned, though, at the responsibility you now have. If you choose the wrong person, instead of funding someone who will cause your investment to grow, you'll be funding a person who is potentially just a drain. Then, some other fabulous student who desperately needs a little help, who is so much like you, may face needless financial hardship and may never even reach his or her goals.

So you read every essay very carefully. You specifically chose the prompt, "How has music changed your life?" so you could really see the role music played in the applicants' mental, emotional, and spiritual lives. Some of the applicants clearly weren't passionate, naming things like, "Music was a great way to meet friends," or "I made money teaching piano."

However, as you're flipping through stacks of essays on your kitchen table at midnight, one essay stands out. Even though this girl's grades aren't that great, she clearly loves music with all her heart. Not only has she volunteered at the community center ("Wonderful," you think, "she likes music enough to not even get paid for it!"), but also she is doing everything in her power to be a music teacher in the inner city of Los Angeles. From the list of jobs she's had, you can see she's trying hard but just can't quite make ends meet. Clearly she's dedicated to her goal: she just needs a little financial help.

There you go. She's the one.

You see how this works? Your application isn't evaluated by a machine. It's being read by people who care about you and your future. They want to see your passion, your dreams, and they want to connect with you, to enable you to make a difference. It's by speaking to them—capturing their heart—that you fund college through scholarships.

Love It

What are you going to be better at and spend more time on: something you love, or something you hate? I know, obvious.

Love scholarships, and you'll get scholarships.

I talk a lot about mindset in this book. That's not accidental: your mindset is crucial to funding college successfully through scholarships. If you go into funding college through scholarships with a lousy attitude about how it's the most miserable thing you've ever done and you're convinced you're totally going to hate every minute, that's going to come out in your applications. Not to mention you won't apply for as many, and I can guarantee you lose 100% of the scholarships you don't apply for. A poor attitude is also going to short circuit all the energy and dedication you're going to need to get scholarships. But really—why do you hate it so much?

Think about it.

1. You're potentially making 10 or more times as much money hourly than you would at a minimum-wage job.

2. You'll have little or no debt and so will be freer to do whatever you want after school.

3. You get to write about what you love—your dreams and passions.

4. You can do it all from the comfort of your home, in your bed, eating cookies and brownies and drinking hot chocolate and coffee (though probably not all at once).

5. You can do it at any hour of the day or night, working ahead on some weeks and skipping the process entirely on other weeks.

The list just keeps on going. Applying for scholarships may not have been super *fun*, per se, but it certainly wasn't the worst thing I ever did. It was satisfying, interesting, a puzzle, and a prize—and the best paying job I'll probably ever have.

So change your attitude to jump-start your success. After all, success is possible, and you *can* fund college through scholarships.

Mindset

As I said, funding college through scholarships is primarily a mindset. There are really only three mindsets you can have regarding scholarships:

1. Scholarships will *not* fund college.

Of course, this is silly. You're not interested in this one because you bought this book (unless it was a gift—or perhaps a strong hint?—and you're so bored on a Friday night this is the best you can do, in which case, I'm truly sorry for you).

2. Scholarships will *help* fund college.

This is the mindset most people have toward scholarships, and why virtually none of them succeed in funding all of college through scholarships. Why? Because if you see scholarships as a supplement, you always have another plan to fall back on: your savings, your job, or your parents. In this way, you're just not going to truly commit yourself to winning scholarships like a machine.

3. Scholarships *will* fund college.

Here is one of the biggest secrets to funding college through scholarships: you have to *decide* to do it, and you have to *commit* to doing it. Yes, you're going to be spending some weekends and breaks and late nights applying for these crazy things, but you're also going to walk across that stage at graduation without a cent of debt, or at least with much less debt than you ever dreamed possible.

So as you're reading the rest of this book, don't sabotage yourself by qualifying everything with the thought, *Well, I don't really need to do all this, because I have other ways of paying for school.* No, you don't. As far as I can tell, private scholarships are the *only* way you will go to *any* school you want, study *any* major you want, get *any* grades you want, for as *long* as you want, and not pay one cent of it from your or your family's money.

Time Commitment

There is a saying that goes, "Time is money, but commitment brings success." Well, with scholarships, time is money only *through* commitment to success. Commitment, not just skill, is critical to funding college through scholarships. Commit to this. It's likely the best paying job you'll ever have.

You say you don't have enough time to spend ten hours getting a $1,000 scholarship—but you do have time to spend 20 hours getting a $200 paycheck?

Now, I understand that part of the hesitancy to spend three or five or ten hours on a scholarship is that it is uncertain: that may be ten hours of wasted time if you never get the scholarship. I've had students tell me they'd rather forego the uncertainty entirely and just work minimum wage, because even if the pay is pathetic, it's guaranteed.

This is a legitimate concern, and I see your point. You have better things to do with your time than to write essays that you couldn't care less about regarding soybean growing or ancient Incan history or world peace in the 21st century. That's why I've written this book: so that you can know exactly what scholarships you are most qualified for—even likely to get—and apply for them in a way that is efficient and effective. That way, you exponentially increase your chances of getting a scholarship and aren't wasting time on ones that you probably won't get. In other words, you control scholarships—they don't control you.

Here are some practical strategies you can commit to funding college through scholarships that I used while in college:

1. **Set aside specific time to work on scholarships**. For example, two hours on Saturdays, or every Thursday night. I can't give you a specific time you should allot in your schedule, but I would generally spend a full day searching for scholarships online once every month or two, and then a several hours *each* week after that putting together applications. But really, I didn't limit myself. Every time I had some free time, I'd usually find myself looking for scholarships.

2. **Look at the odds**. No, not every hour you put in will get you a scholarship, but imagine if there were a $100,000 lottery you had a 1 in 5 chance of winning. Of course you would buy tickets! That is how it is for scholarships: with strategic planning, you could potentially win one in five scholarships you apply for. Even if it's 1 in 10, that's still great odds, and add scholarship to scholarship to scholarship, and pretty soon you have a college education paid in full—that's a pretty good lottery. And you don't even have to spend money on tickets!

3. **Have people who will support you**. If your friends and family are making fun of you for all your work, you're going to get discouraged. Find at least one person to push you on and keep you going.

4. **Imagine the rewards**. No debt. No interest. Freedom. The education you always dreamed. It's worth it. You're worth it.

CHAPTER 5:

The Philosophy of Career Goals

There is one part of the scholarship application more critical than anything else. If you get this part right, then scholarships will start raining out of the sky into your lap. Or pretty close to it. What's that part?

It's you.

You have to know *why* your life plans are:

1. Your heart passion, and

2. Will change the world

Why? Because scholarships aren't actually scholarships: they're people. You win scholarships by touching the people who are giving them out, and those people want to fund people who desire to do great things. That doesn't mean you can't change your mind or your plans in a week, month, or year, but it does mean you need to know your own story deeply: how you became the person you are today, and who you'd like to be in the future.

Now, that doesn't mean you need to be going into what most people consider to be "humanitarian" fields, fields such as medicine, social work, church ministry, or teaching. You could be doing business, or garbage collecting, or quantum physics, or underwater basket weaving—it really doesn't matter. What matters is *why* you are passionate about that field, *why* it is your heart's desire, and *why* it's going to change the world for the better.

Philosophical Thinking

The easiest way to fund college through scholarships is if your quest is fueled by your desire to fund an incredible adventure: the adventure of your life. This requires some deep thinking. It requires you to take a philosophical look at your life and plans and dreams and see to the core of why they are important. So you want to be an architect? It's not just because you enjoy planning, is it? Do you love creating beauty through architecture? Do you love providing a safe haven for parents and their families? Do you love the nurturing community that arises out of a central building for a town? Find what it is you're passionate about in the things you love, and then find what makes your passion your mission. In other words, find what makes you come alive.

"Don't ask yourself what the world needs. Ask yourself what makes you come alive and then go do that. Because what the world needs is people who have come alive."

~Howard Thurman

Actually, applying for scholarships and thus articulating your passions, joys, and the place you see beauty in the world can be life changing. For example, let's say you always thought you were going to be a pediatrician when you grew up, and so you found a scholarship for prospective pediatricians. As you explore why being a pediatrician is your mission and passion and joy, you start realizing you're really struggling. All you can think about is how you truly love being outdoors. If someone asked you why nature was important you could immediately spout off 20 reasons, but medicine—you draw a blank. Your answers about why you love medicine are true, thoughtful, maybe even noble. But they're not from your heart—they're from your brain.

That's *good*. That's a sign that your God-given passion may not be in medicine. That's *okay*. Creation is wonderful, too. So instead, look into what you could do that makes you come alive in nature—that is where you should be.

You may protest, "But I don't know what I want to do with my life!" Don't be afraid if you don't have a certain profession in mind. You *do* have an idea of what you want to do. Why? Because I *know* you have passions and joys. I *know* there are things you love. Imagine if you were entirely "selfish" for a moment, and the only reason the world exists is to bring you as much joy as possible. Now, what would you do? What would make you so gloriously happy you would feel as if you were living a dream?

Find that. Find that dream, because that is where you will come alive. That is what you're supposed to do with your life.

It is not that those dreams will always come true, but to live fully, that passion and joy needs to hold a significant place in your life, and thus in your essays. If you have nothing you are looking forward to in life—nothing that you love about going to college—nothing that makes you shiver with excitement when you look ahead to the next six months or the next six decades—then you need to stop writing essays and start thinking more about your life instead.

That doesn't mean you don't take odd jobs to support yourself, or that you don't make sacrifices. It is just that there is a place out there where your passion meets the world, and you should always be moving toward that place. Theologian Frederick Buechner said, "Vocation is where our greatest passion meets the world's greatest need." Or he once put it another way: "The place God calls you to is the place where your deep gladness and the world's deep hunger meet." Find your deep gladness, your greatest passion: that is the most significant service you can ever give the world.

My Story

Several years ago I anticipated starting a ranch that would rescue horses and pair them with disadvantaged teens to provide both with a place of hope and healing. I was going to do that because I loved horses, and I needed some way to "help the world" through them; I figured working with teens was suitably noble. However, I really wasn't happy with that direction. Finally, one night I became so frustrated I stomped into my room, flipped open my laptop, and madly typed out a five-page rant about what I truly wanted to do with my life and what made me truly happy.

What was it? Nothing the world would exactly consider "noble." As an equestrian, actress, and model, I wanted to act and model with horses in movies and photo shoots, traveling around the world wrangling for films and working with horses. That was a far cry from my camp for troubled teens, but it was what I would do if the world were all about me.

Just one day later, I decided that was the path I was going to follow; I needed to live my life fully alive. As I developed my plans over the years, that original dream morphed and changed into artistic horsemanship marketed through film and photo shoots: my current business of Cambria Horsemanship (**www.cambriahorsemanship.com**), and there is nothing I would rather be doing with my life. And someday, if something else would make me more alive, I will add that in or pursue that instead.

Why do I mention this? Because wrangling horses for films is not exactly the first thing people think of as a humanitarian field. But it was for me—in it, in my unique horsemanship style, I saw a better, more artistically beautiful world for horses and humans, something that was critically important to me. I expressed that in my scholarship essays, and the scholarship providers felt my passion. I won those scholarships.

So go on a walk in the summer woods—grab a cup of tea by the fire—go shoot some baskets—do whatever you need to think deeply about what makes you come alive. Because if you don't know that, you won't be able to fund college through scholarships.

CHAPTER 6:

On Searching and Spreadsheets

Timeline

When should you start looking for scholarships?

You're too late already.

Not to be a downer, but unless you're, oh, five years old, you're probably already behind on the scholarship search. (Actually, if you're five years old and reading this, don't worry about scholarships, because you'll probably be done with college by the time you're 12, anyway.) There are scholarships starting for students as young as elementary school, and the fabulous thing is—*virtually no one knows that!* Most people think of scholarships as something only seniors in high school apply for, but that is one of the biggest mistakes you can make.

Now, if young students do win one of these scholarships and don't know where they want to go to college yet (understandable, considering most 5th graders haven't even decided if they prefer macaroni and cheese or hot dogs), how the money is distributed is up to the scholarship provider. Some send you a check directly, and others will hold onto it until you decide to what college you're going to attend.

In an ideal world, then, start searching for scholarships in elementary school. More scholarships become available when you reach middle school, and, of course, the majority of them are available in high school. Therefore, no matter how old or young you are, start looking now. Even if you don't intend to apply until you're a high school freshman (though that would be silly), start *looking* for scholarships before then.

Why? Let's say you decide to wait until your freshman year of high school to apply for scholarships. Well, it takes a little while to get the hang of it, and it's easy to miss scholarships, so it takes you a full month before you have a list of ones you want to apply for. Well, in that full month you may have already missed a lot of deadlines—not to mention the deadlines that were over the previous summer! That's why you want to look for scholarships a year in advance.

The advantage of finding and applying for scholarships so early is that there are very few applicants for those scholarships, because no one thinks of looking for them that early. Funding college through scholarships is all about finding scholarships you are qualified for *and* for which there are few competitors, so scholarships for 9th, 10th, and 11th graders are perfect for that.

But no matter how old you are, look constantly for scholarships—at least once a month. New scholarships pop up all the time, so you simply cannot look once and think you're done for the rest of your college career. There is no worse feeling than finding a scholarship you are ultra-qualified for and yet soundly missing the deadline because you just didn't find it in time.

Also, don't stop looking for scholarships just because it's summer. Many scholarship applications are due throughout the summer or early in the fall, and it's important to find and apply for them when most other applicants are tanning on the beach (or, bring your laptop to the beach and tan while you apply—how many jobs combine great pay *and* a great tan?).

In fact, summer is the perfect time to *ramp up* your scholarship search. Once school starts, you're going to be busy with the two hundred activities you've overcommitted to, and it will be a lot harder to carve out time to work on scholarships. Therefore, apply for as many scholarships as possible throughout the summer—even if the deadlines are months away—to save time later. Remember, I'm all about both saving time and working efficiently.

Keeping Organized

I know you may barely be able to keep your jeans organized by color, but if there's one thing you're going to need to fund college through scholarships, it's organization. I kept organized through Excel spreadsheets, but you can do it any way you want: spiral notebooks, three-ring binders, Word documents, scrapbooks, smoke signals. But make sure it's easy to keep up!

I definitely think this is easiest done in an Excel workbook. Your workbook will have several pages to it (if you're not familiar with Excel and "workbook" and "sheets," or they sound suspiciously like an algebra assignment, just Google "Excel tutorial," and you'll be set):

1. **Yearly scholarship sheet**

These are the sheets that will keep track of each of your scholarships. Make one for each year, with each sheet having all your scholarships categorized with the following:

- Name

- Amount

- Website/contact information

- Deadline (including type of deadline, whether it's "postmark by" or "arrive by")

- Number of references needed

- Number and type of transcripts needed (ex., high school, college)

- If it's on Zinch (more on that later)

- Anything else you deem helpful

Then, I found it helpful to color coordinate in any way that makes sense for you, such as red for scholarships you didn't win, blue for scholarships you won, yellow for scholarships you've skipped, and green for scholarships you've applied for. Remember to double and triple check your details, because this is your master sheet, and if you record something like a deadline wrong, it could be a disaster!

When you're looking for scholarships, as soon as you find one that you like, just put it on the spreadsheet! For example, here's what your yearly scholarship sheet might look like:

NAME	WHAT'S LEFT	AMOUNT	WEBSITE	DEADLINE	TYPE	TRANSCRIPT	REFERENCES	ZINCH
applied								
won								
didn't win								
skipped								
Busy Bees Scholarship	DONE	500	www.fakebusybeeswebsite.com/scholarshi p	15-Jan	Postmark	2, high school + college	0	yes-applied
Colorado Bug Collectors Grant	DONE	1000	www.fakecoloradobugs.com/scholarship	21-Jan	Arrive by	0	3 (leadership, bugs, academic)	yes-applied
Piano Teachers Assoc. Scholarship	application, reference, essay, transcript	5000	www.fakepianoteachers.com/scholarship	20-May	Arrive by	3	1 (academic)	no
Minnesota Movie Watcher's Scholarship	references	1000	www.fakeilovemovies.com/scholarship	15-Jun	Postmark	1	2 (any)	yes-not applied
Procrastinators Unite Scholarship	essay, SAT documentation	1500	www.fakeilldoitlater.com/scholarship	30-Jun	Postmark	1, plus SAT	0	no
I'd Rather Not Apply Scholarship	application, essay, 2 references, transcript	2250	www.fakeidratherbeskeeping.com/scholars hip	5-Oct	Arrive by	1	2 (employer, professor)	no

When that year comes to a close, make a copy of that sheet and rename it for the next year so that you have all those scholarships again in your database for the coming year. Why? Some scholarships permit you to apply—and win—year after year. But be sure to go back to all the websites at the beginning of the year and double check the deadlines and other details to ensure nothing has changed.

2. College expenses sheet

If you're going to pay for college through scholarships, clearly you have to know how *much* you need to pay. Figure out all of your expenses, including the following:

- Tuition
- Room
- Meal plan
- Books, supplies, and equipment
- Fees
- Travel/vehicle expenses (for commuting or visiting home)

This is your total cost of college. Have your expenses on one side of the sheet and your scholarship income on the other. Set up an Excel formula to add all your scholarship income and subtract all your expenses. As soon as it hits $0, you'll have funded college through scholarships. (This is made a bit more complicated through taxes, however, which is why I have a section on that later.)

An example of this sheet might look like this:

2009-2010			Middle Earth University Cost:	
Honors scholarship from Middle Earth University	11500	-	Tuition	23795
Honors scholarship from Middle Earth University	1000		Meals	3000
Nazgul Conservation Fund Grant	2500		Room	4480
One Ring Replication Scholarship	2500	-	Books	300
Support for Moria Scholarship	1500	-	Fees	200
Legolas Archery Training School	1700			
Shire State Grant	4475			
Gandalf Apprentice Fund	2500			
TOTAL	27675			
NEED TO PAY	4100		TOTAL	31775

3. References sheet

You need to have a large bank of potential references to draw upon for writing references for your scholarships. Why so many? Because you'll be applying for so many scholarships you don't want to burn out any one reference. Therefore, find a minimum of two references that fit *each* of the following categories:

- Employment
- Academic

- Leadership
- Spiritual/religious
- Hobbies (ex., if you're an avid musician, you'll need someone to attest to your musical skills)

Then, contact each of those references to ask if they would be willing to write reference letters for you if need be. You may not draw upon every one of those people, but you'll have them available.

For example:

High School	College	Church	Horses	4-H	Piano
Samwise Gamgee	Tom Cruise	Bill the Pony	Blaise Pascal	Elmo	Chuck Norris
Pocahontas	George Washington		Jason Bourne	Barney	
	Oprah			Rin Tin Tin	

4. Future scholarships sheet

Keep a list of all scholarships you aren't qualified for yet but will be in the future, such as a scholarship just for college seniors, for graduate school, or for studying abroad. Having a page specifically for these scholarships will save you time and make you money in the future when you're ready to apply for them.

CHAPTER 7:

Finding Scholarships

By far, the most common question I'm asked about scholarships is, "Where do you *find* them all?" Sadly, there is no scholarship fairy who will drop them in your lap. Finding scholarships is probably the most time consuming part of applying for scholarships; it took me about one full day (probably eight hours) per month. Thankfully, it's not hard, and you may even be able to do it while watching a movie. (Maybe…)

There are three main places you find scholarships:

1. Scholarship search engines
2. Google
3. Other

Scholarship Search Engines

These are websites like FastWeb.com and Scholarships.com where you plug in your information, such as gender, year in college, and interests, and the search engine gives you a list of scholarships that match your qualifications. There are several advantages of scholarship search engines:

- They're relatively easy, saving you time
- Scholarship providers often know about them, so the larger databases have many scholarships uploaded onto them
- There have scholarships you won't find anywhere else

However, there are significant disadvantages to scholarship search engines.

- They're recommended by every college and high school in the country, so the larger ones, such as FastWeb, are inundated with applicants. This means you'll have to fight to the death against hundreds of applicants for every scholarship. Those are terrible odds.
- Scholarship providers have to upload the scholarships, so if the people upload them improperly, make typos in the names, or, the worst, don't know about the search engines or choose not to upload to the search engines, you'll never find their scholarship.
- Filling out the profile forms can be time consuming.
- Many of the search engines have few scholarships to offer and/or provide inapplicable matches (I have a database reviewing over 25 search engines later on in this book to help you not waste time on those engines).
- It's difficult to find specific "niche" scholarships.

Bottom line, you should definitely use a few prominent search engines, but do *not* let those be where your scholarship search ends. Unfortunately for most students, it is; those search engines are all they know about, so they're continually discouraged by the lack of applicable scholarships and/or the overwhelming amount of bloodthirsty competition for each one—and they don't fund college through scholarships.

When you do use scholarship search engines, here are a few tips to make it more successful:

1. Pick a few good search engines to focus on (I suggest **www.fastweb.com, www.scholarships.com**, and **www.zinch.com**).

2. Carefully fill out your profile. I know this takes a while, but if you mess it up here, the website won't be able to effectively match you to scholarships (and they may already be hard pressed to make good matches so don't make it worse).

3. Check the scholarships on each search engine once a month at minimum, as scholarships are continually added to them.

4. There is usually an option on each scholarship to "hide" or delete it from your scholarship search results. Do this right away for every scholarship you aren't applying for so your results in future months aren't cluttered by inapplicable scholarships.

It's critical that you check out Zinch (**www.zinch.com**). They are a scholarship search engine, student social media site, blog, and student-college connector. But beyond all that, they do one more thing that changes everything: they double the dollar amount of your scholarships. Here's how it works: Zinch posts a list of scholarships on their site; students fill out a Zinch profile, search for scholarships, and mark the ones for which they applied. If it turns out they win one of those scholarships for which they applied, Zinch has a $100,000 fund of money (at least as of this writing) that they use to match that scholarship for the student—doubling the money.

And it doesn't stop there. Through Zinch, you can also...

- **Mooch**: If a friend signs up for Zinch through your referral, you win the same dollar amount of any scholarship they win without lifting a finger!

- **Submit**: If you submit to them a scholarship that isn't in their database, you get a $5 Amazon gift card. Okay, this isn't huge, but you're going to be coming across many scholarships in the coming days, so why not make a few extra bucks along the way?

Zinch is a tremendous service, is not a scam, and the staff are extremely helpful. Be sure whenever you apply for any scholarship, check to see if it's on Zinch, and if it is, mark that you applied! That is the easiest way to make more money through scholarships, and Zinch was a huge player in my ability to fund college through scholarships.

However, you can't end your scholarship search with these search engines. That's what everyone else does. And you're not everyone else.

Google

There are really two keys to winning scholarships consistently. You want to find the scholarships:

1. You are highly qualified for, and
2. No one else knows about.

Basically, you want to be super qualified and have no competition. This raises your chances of getting that scholarship from a shot in the dark to a shot with a sniper rifle in broad daylight with no wind at point-blank range. It's efficient, it's easy, and it will help you get you money.

So, to do that, and do what no one else is doing—fund college through scholarships—you have to go where no one else is going: Google (or Yahoo, Bing, GoodSearch, or any other Internet search engine you like). The vast majority of the scholarships most applicable to you (and with the lowest number of competitors) are not on the scholarship search engines, as the scholarship provider doesn't know about the search engines, doesn't care, or doesn't want to pay to be on there.

However, the scholarship will probably be listed on that provider's website. So how do you find them? Start with a list. A very long list that includes everything that:

- You do and are good at

- You do and wish you were good at

- You don't do but want to do

- You like

- You don't like but are good at

- You've won

- You're involved in

- Relates to you (ex., hometown, religion, political party, environmental sentiments)

- Is unique to you (ex., birth defect, very tall, adopted, rural upbringing)

- Your parents and grandparents have done (ex., club involvement, military, vocations, employers)

As another example, pretend you're Joe. Here is Joe's initial list of words that he might start with (per the above bullet points), though he'll constantly be adding to the list:

Music, piano, violin, band, orchestra, 1st chair violin, football, sports, linebacker, quarterback, honors student, 3.5 GPA, low-income family, 4-H, bird calling, hunting, rock climbing, reality TV, FFA, NRA, Sigma Tau Delta, Evangelical Free Church, Christian, Protestant, Hispanic, Republican, conservative, African aid, traveler, study abroad, green, organic, conservationist, scoliosis, left handed, curly hair, only child, private school, Minnesota Legion, army, Vietnam War, veteran, Cargill, mechanic.

Then, find all of the synonyms or related terms you can think of for each of those words, plus every college major that relates to those things.

For example, one of those words for me was "horse"—I'd ridden since I was five years old and was passionate about the equine industry. So these were my synonyms or related terms:

Equine, equestrian, horse training, stable, ranch, farm, circus, animal, horseback, horsemanship, livestock, pony, ponies, horses, dressage, jumping, natural horsemanship, horse showing, Tennessee Walking Horses, Andalusian

Majors related to horses might be:

Vet, veterinary, vet tech, agribusiness, agriculture, livestock, equine management

Keep going, making a list of synonyms for each of those words. What do you do, now, with this unimaginably huge list?

You start Googling. You Google every one of those words *along with the words* "scholarship," "grant," "fellowship," "contest," "college," and "award." Spend time on each one of those searches, going through several pages of search results, because not all the scholarships will come up on the first page. (If you're really obsessed, you can do the whole process using more than one search engine.)

I know this seems like an insanely huge amount of work. That's both right and wrong. It is a huge amount of work. But it's not insane. It's really smart, because it's how you're going to find the scholarships you're both really qualified for and no one else knows about. And those are almost always the easiest scholarships to win.

Other

Not to be depressing, but not all scholarships are on the Internet. However, the non-Internet scholarships are excellent prospects for you to win, because most other students are only going to look on the Internet. So, if you can find the scholarships not listed online, you'll have far less competition for them.

Here are a few more places to look:

1. **Your parents' work**. Often employers have scholarships available for their employees' students.

2. **Military branches**. There are dozens of scholarships available to service members and their children or grandchildren, particularly if the service member was injured, served in active duty, or was killed in combat. Look these up online or through the military branch you're involved in.

3. **Word of mouth**. Ask students, teachers, friends, colleges, and admissions counselors in your area about scholarships they know about and may be available to you.

4. **E-mail lists and forums**. Find Yahoo Groups, Facebook groups, and forums applicable to your interests and post on them, asking about scholarships available for students in that particular hobby or interest.

5. **High school guidance center**. Your high school can be a great resource of scholarships your peers have won in the past. They may know some very specific scholarships for students in your geographic area or even high school as well.

Be creative! The more places you can ask and search for scholarships, the better your chances are at finding ones no other students have found.

CHAPTER 8:

Choosing the Right Scholarships

After all that searching, you are going to have dozens—even hundreds—of scholarships for which you are qualified and could potentially apply. Obviously, you can't apply for all of them, or else you'll be so busy *funding* college you'd never have time to *go* to college. Besides, it's not like applying for scholarships is going to be your new favorite hobby; you might as well at least try to control the level of discomfort. So which ones do you choose? Or, in other words, how do you become as efficient as possible so you can apply for as few scholarships as possible while still funding college?

There are essentially three kinds of scholarships—those for which:

1. You're not qualified
2. You're technically qualified
3. You're fabulously qualified

You're Not Qualified

Well, this is pretty self-explanatory. You're a guy and the scholarship is for girls. Or, the scholarship is for Martians, and you were born on Pluto (or so your brother tells you). You're not qualified. Don't apply. Duh.

You're Technically Qualified

These are the scholarships that can suck away your life (or so it seems). They're generic and are generally found on sites like FastWeb, often saying something like, "Write 300 words on your life goals," or, "Tell how your dreams will change the world." It's true, you can definitely write 300 words on your life goals. But so can three thousand other applicants who have no interest in putting forth the effort necessary to find those hidden scholarships that are better matched to you anyway, and for which, therefore, there will be much less competition.

Skip these scholarships. Really. I mean, if you truly love applying, go ahead, it's better than a lot of other things you could be doing. Like robbing banks, for one. But honestly, they're not worth your time. Why? First, because of the sheer number of applicants. Your odds are just very low, and the potential for your application being lost under the mountains of other applications is quite high.

Second, it is very likely you will be one-upped by someone whose story is more melodramatic or more of a tearjerker than yours. It doesn't matter if you've single-handedly saved your community from a blizzard in the middle of Alaska. Someone else will have saved his or her community from a blizzard in the middle of the Sahara Desert. Or survived terminal boredom, or rescued orphan ladybugs in the Amazon. Don't get me wrong, those are all wonderful things—it just means, in a generic application with hundreds of competitors, the odds of your story being the most dramatic, in the writing style the scholarship providers most enjoy, and with the specific (unknown) focus they want is very low.

This also applies to scholarships that ask for an essay on a very specific subject—soybeans, world peace, Chinese government, feminism. For example, I once applied for a scholarship on cancer. The requirement was to write an essay about this man who had survived cancer and apply the lessons you learned from him to your own life. "I can do that!" I thought brightly. Many hours and days later, I had written a brilliant essay on cancer and the man who survived it. I didn't get the scholarship.

Why? Not because my writing was terrible (I hope), but because there would certainly have been an applicant who had personal experience with cancer—perhaps her mother, grandfather, or even herself. She would've been able to write a far more touching story about cancer than I ever could have, as I had never truly experienced it. Therefore, she would be more likely to win the scholarship over me. So for those kinds of scholarships, unless you have a burning passion for or life experience with the subject, it's probably better to invest your time and energy elsewhere.

So be careful and be efficient. Don't waste time on scholarships you probably won't get.

You're Fabulously Qualified

These are the holy grail of scholarships, the ones you dream about at night and journal about during the day. When you find them, you feel like your life has just become complete. (In other words, they're like dark chocolate.)

You'll know them when you find them—they are asking for applicants who fit your description perfectly, maybe someone who wants to be a professional concert violinist, or lives in Iowa on a dairy farm, or wants to go to the University of Timbuktu and study synchronized skydiving while living on a 184.2 acre oyster farm with two sisters and a one-eyed pet parakeet named Freddy Bob.

What more can I say? You find these, you put your life on hold to apply. They're what you've been waiting for.

CHAPTER 9:

10 Steps to an Amazing Scholarship Essay

Maybe you're an English major, and you'd rather write than sleep. Maybe you're not an English major and writing is the textbook definition of cruel and unusual punishment. Either way, you'll probably have to change your writing style a bit to write a fabulous scholarship essay—but take heart! In many ways it's the easiest essay you'll ever write.

Just because it's easy doesn't mean you should blow it off, though, because it's one of the most critical parts of your application. First, you need to know what you'll be writing about. Here are a few generic essay prompts I've come across:

1. Write 500 words on your life goals.

2. In no more than three pages, discuss how college will help you attain your future plans.

3. In 50 words or less, summarize your career plans and dreams.

As you can see, the length of the generic essay can vary tremendously, anywhere from 50 words to five or more pages. For this reason, you will want to develop several versions of your generic essay so you'll always have the perfect one ready. I suggest beginning with writing a 100-word, 500-word, 1,000-word, and 3,000-word scholarship essay. I know that sounds like a lot, but it's not so bad: just start with the 3,000-word essay and keep paring it down until you have all four. It's like writing one essay and just summarizing it in a few others.

But how do you make those essays good? Well, I have ten guidelines I used on every one of my scholarship essays that helped them stand out—and allow me to fund college through scholarships. Each guideline is developed to systematically prove to the scholarship provider that you are the best, most reliable, dedicated, proven, humanitarian, and likely-to-succeed candidate out there for their scholarship.

1. Obvious

Scholarship providers will be skimming your essay. There is just no way around it; *you* try reading 50 essays a day for five days straight and see if you don't start skimming! For this reason, you need to have an extremely clear thesis statement (ex., "My life goals are three fold…") with paragraphs clearly labeled ("The first part of my life goals includes…"). You can even number, bold, or italicize if you feel it helps (just don't go overboard; this isn't a 6th grade writing assignment). The key is, if someone were just to skim the "headlines" of your essay, would they know what it was about?

Also include summary sentences, even if the word count is tight. At minimum, restate the thesis at the end of your essay, and if you're not tight on words, restate the topic sentence of the paragraph at the end of each paragraph. In essence, you're trying to "tell them what you're going to tell them, tell them, then tell them what you just told them." That way they'll never forget your essay!

It's going to seem overboard to label sentences "First," "Second," Third," and so on, but remember, you're not writing for your poetry instructor: this is a scholarship essay. Different rules apply. Make it so obvious you think you're going to throw up, and then you're probably good.

2. Comprehensive

You know all those times you bit your lip and didn't tell the world all the awesome things you've done? Here's your chance to spill it all, and it's not bragging—it's just not hiding anything. (Bragging is something you should avoid and has that pompous, "I'm-so-amazing-you-can't-believe-it" feel. Scholarship providers won't want to fund that sort of person.)

Don't be shy! In the ideal, comprehensive essay, you'll want to have one paragraph each—at a minimum—on the following topics:

➢ What you intend on doing with your life in a philosophical sense—your vision and dreams

➢ What your specific future plans and goals are to achieve that vision, including 1-year, 5-year, and 10-year plans; no, you won't know every detail, but this is your time to dream—what would your ideal life look like?

➢ Steps you've already taken to achieve your vision

➢ Activities and impressive accomplishments you've gained in working toward your vision

➤ Why that vision and its accompanying plans and goals matter to the world (How will they help people? How do they fulfill your dreams for a better world?)

➤ How the scholarship will be used, and why you need it (be specific!)

➤ Why you will succeed in life (and in fulfilling your vision)

➤ Why you stand out and are better than the other applicants (be careful here, no putting others down!)

Now, of course, you won't be able to include all of this in every essay (at least not that 50-word one…). But this comprehensive mindset is one you want to keep hold of, and even if it's just a sentence touching on each bullet point mentioned here, that will be enough to really impress the scholarship providers!

3. Perfect

In high school, maybe even college, teachers generally allow you an error or two (or more!) per page of your essay without docking you points. Not so with scholarship essays. As sad as it is, scholarship providers are looking for reasons to dump your application and choose someone else—after all, they have to wade through dozens or even hundreds of applications, and applicants have to be eliminated somehow.

Therefore, the grace allowance of errors for your scholarship essay is a whopping "zero." Punctuation, grammar, spelling, sentence structure, colons, semi-colons—they all need to be perfect. Even if you're a grammar guru, have another guru proofread it. If you're not so much a guru, well, maybe have *several* gurus proofread it.

4. Applicable

Here's where you can really stand out, because this is something almost no student does. It'll take time and research, but it's worth it.

What you want to do is research the scholarship provider to find qualities they admire and respect. For example, I once applied for a scholarship hosted by a certified fraud examiner's society—people who look into businesses to make sure they have ethical practices. Now, my career plans didn't include becoming a fraud examiner, and I didn't hide that in my essay, though I highly respect the profession.

However, I did go on their website and learn that the organization wanted their fraud examiners to have an interest in business, high standards in morality, ethics, and accuracy, and be able to correct failings in those high standards when they were found. Therefore, I crafted my essay around those qualities, giving examples from my life, goals, and plans how I fulfilled every one of those virtues. I also specifically highlighted the fact that these were qualities of a fraud examiner—in other words, you don't have to make your research work incognito!

In summary, research the scholarship for which you're applying. Find out what qualities the organization or provider is looking for, what they value, what they would love to see the world look like. Then, craft your essay around those qualities—speak their language.

5. Unique

With all of these rules and guidelines, you may feel a tendency to want to write like a robot, stuffing every possible fact and award into your essay in exactly the right way as perfectly as possible. Don't do that. Remember, you're writing to real people, and those real people want to know you're a real person with your own personality and wonderful uniqueness. You have certain qualities no one else does, and who are you to say those qualities aren't exactly what the scholarship providers are looking for?

Meaning, be yourself. Be beautiful. Be different. Take a risk in how you write—include humor, or philosophy, or your faith. Poke fun at yourself. Write something that will make you real. A "perfect," sanitized essay will never win; you need your essay to stand out among dozens or hundreds not only because it's persuasive, but because you're a real *person*.

For example, take a risk with your opener. Imagine you're a scholarship provider for a moment. You have a stack of 106 essays in front of you, you've gone through 48, and it's 11 p.m. You pick one up:

I want this scholarship because...

Boring.

My name is Sally-Mary Jones and...

Yeah, whatever.

If I get this scholarship, I will...

Yawn.

Fighting aliens with light sabers changed me into a Jedi knight.

What!?

Okay, so, light sabers and Jedis probably won't make it into your scholarship opener, but never underestimate the power of a wild, fascinating scholarship essay starter. Make it *you*. Use a story, movie reference, bizarre quote, radical statement. Be professional, but be risky—*playing it safe does not get you scholarships.*

A startling opener does a few things for you. First, it shocks the essay reader into paying attention; if they pause for even two extra seconds, it has made your essay stand out among dozens.

Second, it makes your story more compelling—suddenly you're a real person with a real personality, not just a robot who wrote the essay because his mom made him.

Finally, it's more fun. If you start with a fun opener, chances are the rest of your essay will follow suit and be enjoyable to read. And think about it: if all else were equal, why wouldn't the scholarship provider choose the essay that is actually entertaining to read?

So say something radical—the boring things have all been said too many times, anyway. Besides, if you're not living life on the edge, you're taking up too much space. (And you won't fund college through scholarships.)

6. Philosophical

If you just talk about your awards, your 13-point life plan, or your intended college degree, you're not going to get many scholarships. Why? Because everyone can come up with a life plan and goals, and everyone can choose a degree. Scholarship providers are giving scholarships because they want to help people—and so they want to help people who are going to help *other* people. Show them how investing in you is going to be a tremendous return on investment, so that by helping you, their money will actually be helping the world.

Now, you don't have to make this up (and I'm certainly not advocating that you do!). Go back to the earlier section in this book on your life goals and plans: how is what you're doing going to change the world? Don't be afraid to be philosophical in your essay; this not only deepens you as a human being, but also shows the scholarship providers that you think and care deeply, both about your life and the lives of others.

By the way, you may not have an isolated paragraph on how what you're doing is world changing; in fact, you may not want to, as it may sound contrived. Instead, a more authentic and impressive way of achieving this is to blend such thoughts throughout your entire essay—references to the greater good your plans and dreams hold for the world or your community.

For example, say you want to teach high school football. You may want to do it because you love sports, and there's nothing wrong with that. But you can go deeper. Explain how your own football coach changed your life, and how you want to pass on his legacy; give examples of your friends changed by sports and how you want to help their children have the same experience; show how playing sports deepens students' character, mind, and body, making them into more fulfilled human beings. Give specifics. Do you want to see your hometown have less crime by giving teenage boys an outlet? Do you want to help your small farm town's youth get football scholarships for college? All of these are ways to show you are thinking outside yourself.

7. Concise

Earlier, I gave you a list of bullet points of everything you should include in your essay. You may be wondering how you can possibly include all that in five pages, much less 100 words. My answer: *be concise*. No matter how concise you think you are, you can always be more so.

For example, let's look at my own thesis statement for my generic essay as it goes from somewhat wordy to increasingly concise:

Galloping across the screen without saddle or bridle, Shadowfax of Lord of the Rings embodies much of my life vision, his mythical connection with people immortalized through film. Indeed, my life vision consists of finding Shadowfax, starting a business in equine liberty training that inspires others through the use of horses in film and photo shoots.

While there is nothing wrong with these sentences, and, actually, they're already relatively concise, see how much shorter they can be made:

Galloping across the screen, Shadowfax embodies much of my life's two-fold vision: (1) to have a business developing equine liberty training that (2) inspires others through its use in film.

I said the same thing—just in a lot fewer words! Now, the second example isn't always ideal. For example, what if I were quite sure the scholarship providers had no idea who Shadowfax was? (By the way, if you don't know, he's Gandalf's gorgeous gray horse in the *Lord of the Rings* books and movies. Don't know who Gandalf is? Stop reading right now and go watch the movies.). However, when you're short on words, you need to learn how to cut.

In fact, you can get a novel on a single page if you really try, and the more concise you are, the more information you'll be able to pack in to explain why you are the best candidate for the scholarship. (If you don't believe me about the novel thing, Google "Book-A-Minute Classics" and prepare to be amazed.)

8. Persuasive

Your essay is supposed to convince the scholarship providers there is absolutely no one better than you for this scholarship. Therefore, the whole essay is an exercise in persuasion and rhetoric. Now, that doesn't mean you're dishonest—it just means you present yourself and your life in the most convincing way possible.

For example, when talking about your goals and accomplishments, give specific examples of what you have done through appealing emotionally (stories, testimonials, examples), logically (facts, numbers, awards), and spiritually (philosophy, dreams). Don't forget to tell stories of how you've changed your own life, changed others, and changed your community. Scholarship providers want to know how you've mattered to this world in the past and will matter to it in the future!

Good rhetoric is specific. Which is more powerful: "I have won a lot of 4-H awards," or, "I have won 33 4-H blue ribbons at the county, regional, and state level over the past six years, competing in 13 divisions, including dog, horse, food and nutrition, and performing arts, honored with three Minnesota State Fair Grand Championships in digital photography, competing against up to 32 other participants"? Yeah, I thought so.

In other words, give details: numbers, awards, years, competitors, and specific proper nouns. The more specific you are, the more you are fleshed out as a real human being who has real accomplishments in the past and is likely to have real accomplishments in the future—and therefore be someone the scholarship provider will want to fund.

9. Interesting

If you don't like your essay, the scholarship provider probably won't. Meaning, you have to love what you're writing about, passionately sharing about your life and dreams and goals—you have to be interested in the subject of your essay. This definitely relates to what I said earlier about discovering your life passions and dreams. The incredible writer C.S. Lewis once said, "Write about what really interests you, whether it is real things or imaginary things, and nothing else."

Sound too good to be true? It isn't—not for scholarship essays. I know you probably think nothing could be more boring than writing 500 words on your life goals, but in fact, in the dozens of scholarship essays I wrote, I found the exact opposite to be the case: those essays were a thrilling opportunity to write about what I loved.

For example, what is your absolute favorite subject, the one you could talk about until midnight and surf the Internet about for hours? Basketball? Flute? Computer programming? Backpacking across Colorado? The best scholarship essays on your life and college goals will revolve around those heart passions. They will focus on the most amazing vision for your life you can think of—what you would dream if the only requirement were that you were utterly happy. And believe me, dreams like those are fun to write about.

As C.S. Lewis said, sometimes you're going to feel like you're writing something imaginary, but then, great people rarely stick to the normal, do they? In that way, writing the perfect scholarship essay is like writing a fairy tale, an action movie, an adventure novel—where you are the star. And what could be more exciting than that?

10. Supported

For number ten, you get a break: this rule has nothing to do with you, and everything to do with the people with whom you surround yourself. You need to be supported when writing so many essays, so have one or two committed people who will read your essays over and over. They're going to read every essay for every scholarship, helping edit, add or remove words, or make it even more fascinating. For me, it was my dad. Every time I applied for a new scholarship, I'd edit my essay, print it out on scratch paper, slap it on the kitchen table, and he'd give it back to me the next day covered in red pen.

After all, you're not going to be reading this essay—the scholarship providers will be. Therefore, it makes sense to have people other than you reading the essay. Others need to understand and love it or the scholarship committee never will. People committed to your education and scholarships will catch errors and give you new ideas you never would have thought of on your own.

Non-Generic Topic Essays

Now, some essays aren't generic and don't ask about your life goals at all. This is the case with the essays of "topic scholarships" such as, "Write about how Martin Luther King, Jr., was an effective leader," or, "Explain how you think world hunger can be solved in your lifetime."

There is a key to nailing these essays: treat them like the generic scholarship essay. Meaning, yes, the scholarship providers want and need you to answer the specific question they're asking, but the purpose of the scholarship hasn't changed: to fund worthy students' educations. So prove you're worthy.

In other words, the key to writing a knockout "topic" essay is to weave in as much of your generic essay as possible to prove you are a fabulous scholarship candidate. For example, take the Martin Luther King, Jr., prompt. You wouldn't just write about King throughout the entire essay. Rather, every time you mention one of his specific leadership principles (with sources, references, and footnotes, of course!) you'd also apply it to your own life. So if one of his qualities was remaining calm under pressure, you'd expand on that, and then give an example from your own life how you have been calm under pressure. And then later, when you highlighted his quality of foresight, you would illustrate its effect on your own life by foresight you are showing about your own future.

Essay Example

Here is a real-life example of one of my generic scholarship essays, just to give you an idea of how I structured mine. It's not perfect, but it may give you a few ideas.

The Truth of a Legend

Galloping across the screen, Shadowfax of the Lord of the Rings films embodies my life vision, his mythical connection with people immortalized through film. Indeed, my life vision is two-fold: (1) to have a business in equine liberty training that (2) inspires others through its use in film.

While most horses are trained through force, the internationally-recognized approach I use is to educate a horse entirely without tack or on a loose line, uniquely combining the two specific horsemanship techniques of "feel and release" and liberty training. This method will be at the core of the business I intend to form, which will, first, teach this method through clinics, lessons, and multimedia, and second, use it to train horses for film.

Indeed, liberty horses in film, such as Flicka or the Black Stallion, penetrate our deepest emotions, impacting people worldwide and awakening our longing for a deeper horse-human connection that has been too long forgotten. I want to further that longing by training horses specifically for that purpose, seeking to specifically train horses as a film wrangler and perform with them as a professional actress. I am passionate enough about both horses and film to pursue them separately; combined, their force is exhilarating.

To do this, I am designing an Interdisciplinary major, combining equine business/management and film studies. I have been accepted at multiple prominent horsemanship schools for internships. Currently, I am building a horse training business, am taking acting training, and am preparing to submit my animals to an animal acting agency. Unfortunately, internships are typically unpaid, building a business is costly, and film shoots and study reduce time for paid work. For these reasons, I am asking for this scholarship.

I have long been on a horsemanship path to achieve this vision. I have been a leader in my 10 years in the 4-H Horse project and a volunteer in giving over 1100 hours to a youth ranch and teaching riding lessons for free. I have been a student in working at seven barns, attending dozens of clinics, showing in over a dozen disciplines, and was invited to study at multiple internationally known horsemanship schools. I have been self-taught in participating in two online schools, studying over 150 hours of DVDs. I have been an entrepreneur in beginning my own business (www.cambriahorsemanship.com) and being an invited presenter at three horse expos.

For film education, I take acting lessons, am involved in college theatre, work with animal on-camera agencies, and am an actress and model both professionally and as a volunteer in charity, student, and independent productions. In academics, although Northwestern offers many advantages, it did not have my desired degree of Entrepreneurship, so I designed it myself within the Interdisciplinary Studies program. This has been an enriching experience as I design schedules, choose classes, research programs, and harmonize financial aid, all while maintaining a 4.00 GPA.

The future holds exciting plans as well. First, I am pursuing training in a prominent local barn, where I anticipate becoming an employed instructor in the coming year. Also, I want to expand my promotion of Cambria Horsemanship to teaching and exhibiting at expos and shows. Finally, I want to take advantage of that promotion by hiring professional services to help make Cambria a viable business.

Ultimately, I believe I will succeed—not just because of my self-motivation and not just because of the personal support I have by professionals in these fields—but because I believe I have a unique vision: a vision of a world where a forgotten connection with horses can be awoken. Indeed, Shadowfax has awed many, but for me, his inspiration goes deeper, for I see him daily in the liberty horses I train. Is he merely a legend? Perhaps. But if so, let my life be dedicated to making this legend live.

CHAPTER 10:

Awards and Activities

There is another element besides the essay most scholarships ask for: your awards, honors, and activities. Meaning, there will be a section on the application form that says something like, "List all your high school and college honors, awards, and activities." This part of the essay is critical—rivaling the essay—but will be a nightmare if aren't prepared for it. Why? Because you won't have any of your honors and awards organized, and you won't be able to remember half of them anyway!

Creating Room

Your first problem will be that applications never seem to give enough room to list all your activities: there you are, filling out their great application, all confident in your skills, and you come to the *Activities and Awards* section. How much space have they given you?

Two lines.

That just isn't enough space to cover all the awesome things you've done in your life. What do you do? There are two options:

1. Try to cram everything in two lines. Unless you're including a magnifying glass with your application, this isn't a good idea.

2. Write the scholarship provider and ask to include extra sheets. This is a good idea.

Sometimes, scholarship providers won't want extra pages, so then you'll just have to summarize (instead of giving every detail, summarize it something like, "45 4-H awards, three MMTA piano championships, five years as Sunday School teacher"). However, most scholarship providers are fine with you including more pages. In that case, just write, "See attached sheets" in the provided lines and staple your extra sheets to the application.

Now, what do you include in those attached sheets? You want to list every award, honor, activity, leadership role, club involvement, and anything else you have ever accomplished, held, or won. Even include unofficial positions and give them official names. For example, at Northwestern College, as part of the honors program, I was assigned a freshman honors student to meet with and help get on her way as a successful honors student. This wasn't official, and it didn't take much time. However, it was still a responsibility, so I named it "Honors Program Mentor" and put it on my activities and awards sheet. Find responsibilities like that to fill out your sheets!

Also, just like the scholarship essay, be very specific. Ban words like "many," "a lot," "some," or "frequently"—use the "Find" feature in your word-processing software to make sure you don't miss even one! Those words don't impress anyone. "Many" may mean "dozens" to you but imply "twice" to the scholarship provider, which would be terribly unfortunate. Therefore, include exact numbers, dates, years involved, roles, and responsibilities whenever possible. Think of it like a résumé on steroids!

How many years back should you go in listing your awards? Focus on college and high school; scholarship providers generally don't care too much about activities before then. The only exception to this is activities you started before high school and carried on into high school. Meaning, I wouldn't put on my sheet that I took ballet when I was five and stopped a year later (despite to this day still remembering how to contort into fifth position), but I would put on there I started taking horseback riding lessons at five and continued taking them through college. Or, as a different example, when I provided the number of 4-H blue ribbons I had won, I also included those won *before* high school.

Organizing Your Awards

Developing these sheets can be horribly overwhelming if you haven't been keeping track of this throughout your life. However, it's worth the effort, and once you have your initial list, it'll be very easy to keep it updated.

Start by going through your scrapbooks, laptop documents, files, photo albums; ask your parents, grandparents, friends; look at 4-H records, diaries, Facebook posts and pictures. Compile every activity, honor, and award you can find and then put them all in a spreadsheet. After that, just keep the list constantly updated: every time you participate in a new club, are interviewed for the school newspaper, or win another award, just put it in your spreadsheet! You'll have an amazing reference library not only for scholarships but also for résumés later on.

The spreadsheet needs to be easy to read. Mine was organized by college on top, high school under, with subheadings of leadership, academics, and athletics. The vertical columns included name, description, years involved, and special awards. However, like the essay, it is important to customize these sheets to match what the application asked for, or what you think the application should have asked for.

Meaning, the application might ask for your leadership, volunteer work, and music-related activities. Therefore, those should be the three categories on your sheets. Or, perhaps the application just asks for "honors and activities," but you know it's a pet-related scholarship. Therefore, you would break up your sheets into pet-related and non-pet-related honors and activities to make it more applicable to the scholarship providers and easier for them to read.

For example, here's a pared-down version of a sample activities and awards sheet:

Frodo Baggins' University and High School Resume for Year 5422 Shire Conservation Scholarship	No.Yrs Involved	Description or Special Awards/Honors	Off -ices Held
Activity			
COLLEGE			
Academics			
Shire University Honors Program	2	3.9+ GPA bracket	
Dean's List, Highest Honors	2	In the 3.9--4.0 grade bracket	
Communications Department Teaching Assistant	2	Manage homework, tutor students, create exams, grade homework, plan/run events, organize	

		instructional materials.	

Leadership			
Entrepreneur: Baggins Ring-Destruction Business (www.destroythering.com)	1	Designed website and blockbuster movie trilogy around my Rings of Power destruction skills and accompanying community building	Gro up Leader
Mentor:			
Fellowship of the Ring	1	Coached new group members in how to relate safely to Rings of Power	
Honors Program	1	Mentored new student in Gandalf's Honors Program	

Volunteer/ Member			
Rivendell Protectionist Club	2	Weekly meetings and bi-annual events and performances promoting sustainable use of Rivendell resources	
Other/short-term volunteering	2	Various organizations: Hobbit Happiness (teaching gardening to disadvantaged Hobbits), Read with Bill (reading program with ponies and dwarves), etc.	

Fine Arts			
Shire University Theatre/Performance:	2	3 showcases/plays/performances, 4 student films, 3 tech crews (spotlight, costume, hair/makeup), 3	Lea d

Local On Camera Industry:	2	Word of Witness dramatized chapels, 2 improv skits, 1 dance, 1 music video 3 full-length feature films, 10 photo shoots, 8 training classes/workshops, 1 industrial, 5 voiceovers, 2 films (only 2 projects paid; rest were volunteer)	Lead
Animals			
Shire Sheepherding Youth of America	4	#3 youth sheep herder in the Shire, competing against 30+ students every year in guiding 10 sheep through a maze while I was blindfolded at night	
Nazgul-training clinic assistant and coordinator (Nazguls Naturally, Art of Nazguls)	3	Help keep clinics running smoothly, handing out paperwork, organizing lunch, cleaning up, etc.	
Invited Opportunities: Middle Earth Sheep Expo Clinician Apprenticeships		Invited to bring my sheep and give demonstrations Asked to teach blindfolded sheep herding clinics Invited to apprentice with three international sheep trainers	Exhibitor Clinican
Athletics/Other			
Mines of Moria Mining Expo	2		Attender
Gardening, hiking, hallucinating	2		

PRE-COLLEGE/HIGH SCHOOL			
Note: Because I was homeschooled my academic activities were often through outside programs.			
Academics			
National Merit Super-Shire Scholar Program Finalist	1		
MEOS (Middle Earth Official Saviors) Awards (speech, projects, drama, animals)	10	80+ blue ribbons (local and state), 60+ (reserve) champions and honorable mentions	
Communication Arts: *Interpretive Reading*	5	9 Championship/Reserve Championships (including State), 1 State Honorable Mention	Local, Regional, State
Communication Arts: *Creative Writing*	5	4 Championship/Reserve Championships	Local, Regional
Shire Area Scholars at Home	10	Participated in activities, meetings, field trips	
"There and Back Again" Book Quizzing	2	International Tournament Team Champion (2x)	Co-Captain
	2	International Tournament Top 5 Quizzer (2x)	
Fine Arts			
Writing			
Foundation for the Nazgul Breeders' and Exhibitors' Contest	1	National Champion	
Sheep Herders International Essay Contest	5	National Champion	

Photography			
Photography, Shire County Fair	8	County Champion	
Photography, MEOS State Fair	4	Blue Ribbon Winner	
Nazgul Photography Contest	3	National Reserve Champion	

CHAPTER 11:

References and Transcripts

References

References are a fun part of your application. Why? Because you don't have to write them. Anything you don't have to do yourself is awesome! But references can also be a stressful part of your application, as they're a lot like group projects: your whole life and success rests entirely on another person and you have absolutely no say in the matter. Life just isn't fair.

Thankfully, you have more control over your references than you do over the members of your group project. First, you can pick them, and you want to ensure you have many to choose from. Therefore, start building relationships now, no matter how young you are. You want professional, personal relationships with as many adults as possible and in as many areas of your life as possible—school, volunteer, leadership, religion, and extracurricular. Keep in mind that most scholarship applications ask for references who have known you for several years and are not related to you.

As you build those deep relationships, don't be afraid to ask the person if someday he or she would be willing to serve as a reference for you. Most likely, the person will be flattered! However, those people are going to need something to comment on in their letters, so make sure you stand out—in a good way. Don't be the student about whom the professor has to write, "I could not recommend this student any more."

As you build up these relationships, keep a list of each person who has agreed to serve as a reference (or you are quite sure would serve as one), probably on another spreadsheet (remember what I said earlier about your Excel workbook?). Categorize them by the area of your life they are most experienced in, such as your volunteer work at church, your academics in high school, or your cross-country skiing.

Why? Because scholarships usually ask for references that relate to a particular area of your life. And even if they don't, you want to give them as close a match as possible. Meaning, if it's a medical-related scholarship, you're going to want your volunteer reference letter to be from your supervisor at the hospital you volunteered at last summer. That will mean a lot more to the scholarship providers than, say, if it is from your music teacher.

Finding Good References

The right references can make or break your scholarship application.

Look at it from the point of view of the scholarship provider: they know you're only using references who will give you a positive review. That teacher you couldn't stand in 10th grade math who gave you a D and relished using that scary red pen? You're obviously not asking him.

So it comes as no surprise that all your references will tell your scholarship provider how great you are, and it's of zero help to your application, because every other reference for every other applicant will be saying the exact same thing. The key is to make your references paint such an amazing picture of you that the scholarship providers see it as a no-brainer to give you the scholarship. The question is, then, how do you make sure your references write unbelievable referrals for you?

Start with these tips:

1. **Make sure they're good writers themselves**. Find some of their writing to examine—not only for basic grammar and punctuation, but also for general style. Is their writing passionate, vivid, and interesting? If so, it'll make your application stand out.

2. **Get as "high-level" references as possible**. Meaning, a reference from the CEO of a company is going to mean a lot more to the scholarship provider than a letter from your best friend from high school. In the world of scholarships, rank and position mean a lot.

3. **Consolidate**. Because you're organized (yes, you are), you know if you'll need three reference letters from the same person within the next six months. Tell the references this in advance so they can do all your letters at once, or, at least, mentally prepare for the fact you'll be asking them for more letters. Also, some references are all right with giving you multiple hard copies of the letter, or even a Word document, so you don't have to come back to them repeatedly. This can be very helpful if you need multiple references from the same person.

4. **Give them your information**. Even if your reference is your mom (bad idea), don't assume she'll know or remember all the amazing things you've done. So provide each reference with an impressive list of your awards, honors, and activities, particularly as they relate to that scholarship.

5. **Give them scholarship information.** Tell them what the scholarship is judging you on (character? spirituality? awards? leadership? volunteer work?) so they can customize the letter to exactly fit what the scholarship provider wants.

6. **Give them specifics.** Is the letter supposed to be one page? Addressed to the scholarship providers? Signed over the flap? Include a business card? Returned to you? Postmarked by a certain day? Give them all the information they need in a clear bullet-pointed or numbered list.

7. **Give them time.** Three weeks minimum is what you should allow for each reference, and the deadline you give them should be at least a week *before* the deadline you have for sending off the entire scholarship packing. Your reference needs to be thinking happy thoughts about you when writing the letter, and if you gave her only 16 hours to write it in—well, those happy thoughts may be pretty nonexistent.

With these guidelines, you should get some pretty great reference letters. Always remember to thank your references profusely, tell them if you won the scholarship, and bring them chocolate and cookies at every possible opportunity. After all, they're helping you fund college through scholarships.

Transcripts

There are few things worse than working yourself to death to get awesome grades on your transcript and then not having the transcript to send in and impress people with. In other words—high schools and colleges can be a little pokey about sending you transcripts after you've requested them. Even if they're not slow, it'll still probably take over a week from the time you request a transcript to the time you actually have it.

Solution? Order a bunch of transcripts (at least ten) at the beginning of each semester, quarter, or trimester (depending on how often your school posts new grades), so you always have plenty of transcripts on hand. At the end of that semester, throw out your old ones, request new ones with your up-to-date grades, and start again. Yes, I know it's odd asking your registrar for ten transcripts at a time, and I often wondered if my registrar figured I'd gone off my rocker, but, hey—I was getting paid $1,000 an hour, so I'd say a little weirdness was justified.

Many scholarships also ask for your SAT, ACT, and PSAT scores, and even if the application doesn't ask for them, if your scores were impressive, put them on the application! But be aware that some scholarships want official documentation of those scores. Therefore, find out if the scores are listed on your high school transcript and, if not, find how you can get official copies of your test results so you'll have them ready for any application. Your college or high school guidance counselor should be able to help you with this.

CHAPTER 12:

Graduate School Scholarships

Don't Ignore It

I'm not only about saving money—I'm about saving time. Getting your bachelor's degree may be as far as you want to go, but, no matter how sure you are you won't be going to grad school, don't totally dismiss the idea—at least not yet.

After all, you have no idea the kind of person you're going to be in four years, and you may well discover that to fulfill your dreams you'll need a master's or doctorate. Wouldn't it be nice if you could make that decision without having to worry about where the money would come from?

Well, you can make that a reality. Remember how on your master Excel workbook, you have a sheet for keeping track of scholarships you're not qualified for yet? Well, make sure you include potential grad school scholarships, fellowships, and research grants on that sheet. That way, if on the off chance you decide to go to grad school, you already have a list of free money ready to go.

What to Search For

How do you apply for grad school scholarships? Everything you've read in this book regarding undergrad scholarships applies to grad school ones as well. While at the time of writing there were no specific scholarship search engines for grad students, there are grad school scholarships on all the traditional search engines. Although there are generally fewer private scholarships available for grad school students (simply because fewer people go to grad school), the advantage is that when you find a good grad school scholarship, there will be fewer applicants for it! And remember, winning scholarships is all about finding scholarships you're very qualified for and have little competition.

Unlike undergrad scholarships, most grad school scholarships come from professional organizations related to your major and/or career, such as marketing, or nursing. This is particularly true if your career path always requires higher education (ex., lawyer or dentist). There are huge numbers of scholarships out there for popular fields such as medicine or teaching.

Often graduate "scholarships" are in the form of fellowships or research grants, so they don't always directly apply to tuition. However, they'll still be instrumental in helping reduce the financial strain on you as you work toward your higher degree. Therefore, when searching on the web for scholarships, be sure to use the words "grant," "research grant," and "fellowship" along with your traditional "scholarship."

The Application

First, update all your references to be people who knew you from your undergrad years—references from high school are too distant. After all, *someone* must've known you in college. When at all possible, get references who are the heads of departments, research programs, honors programs, or are in any other position of authority. Make sure to let them know you're applying for grad school scholarships so they know to emphasize the quality of your undergrad work and that you'll hold up well in a master's program.

Next, update your awards and activities sheets. Grad school scholarships may still ask for these, but you'll want to place a high emphasis on your undergrad activities as well as any and every activity and award related to your field of study. No longer are you an "undecided major" in undergrad, and no longer is uncertainty about your career acceptable. You definitely have a career path now, so you need to prove why you are the best student on that particular path for that particular scholarship.

Finally, remember to strongly emphasize your career choice, path, dreams, and the philosophy behind it in your essays. If you're going for your master's or doctorate, *you* know why you're passionate about that field, but the scholarship provider needs to know it, too.

CHAPTER 13:

Making Scholarship Deadlines

How to Never Win a Scholarship

There is one way to ensure your scholarship will never get chosen, and it's 100% effective:

Miss the deadline.

That about sums it up. Send your application in too late, and you'll never get chosen.

But don't despair. Remember that phrase, "Everything I need to know I learned in kindergarten?" Well, that holds true here, because if you remember Goldilocks and the Three Bears, you'll never have a problem with scholarship deadlines.

Why? Because you shouldn't apply too early, and you definitely shouldn't apply too late. The key is to apply right on time.

Why shouldn't you apply too early? Because scholarship providers are people, too. If I gave you a paper and said, give it back to me in five minutes, chances are, in five minutes you'd still have the paper, right? Sure. But let's say I gave it to you and said, give it back to me in five months? There is a lot better chance you'd have lost it or forgotten about it.

The same is true if you apply so early your application gets to the scholarship provider many months ahead of time. Even more, if you've applied months in advance, you'll likely to have some great life experiences, honors, activities, or awards that will occur during those months but you won't be able to include on your application because you already sent it in.

But if you apply too late, there's a chance your essay won't arrive in time, or, at best, will slide in at the last moment and not make a very good impression (not to mention causing you to turn a lot of hair gray as you stress about it arriving on time).

Therefore, the best time for your application to arrive is one to three weeks before the actual deadline. That means there is no way your application won't get there in time—no matter how slow the post office is—but you also had the maximum amount of time to perfect your application.

Know the Real Deadline

There is a caveat to all this, however. You need to know the deadline. "Well, that's silly," you say, "Of course I know the deadline!" Fine.

Postmark or arrive-by?

Yeah, I thought so. There is a tremendous difference between the two. Let's say the deadline is June 1. Some scholarships have a postmark date, meaning, if it's to be postmarked June 1, as long as the office slams its little stamp on the envelope by June 1, no matter how many days it takes to actually arrive, your application is safe.

However, some scholarships have an arrive-by deadline, meaning, your application has to be in their hands by June 1. This is harder for you to plan for, because what if it gets lost in the mail? What if there is a holiday on the day you were going to send it? What if your car runs out of gas on the way to the post office?

If it's a postmark deadline, no worries, you can handle that. If it's arrive-by, I generally gave my applications a week to be sent anywhere in the United States. If there is any concern about your essay arriving in time (or even if there isn't!), it's a great idea to e-mail the scholarship provider telling them your application is on its way. E-mail is preferable to a phone call in this case, as it gives them a dateable "paper trail" so it's proven you contacted them before the deadline. This not only helps them remember your name (and thus your application when they're judging them) but also gives you a backup in case the worst happens and your essay is a day late—because of the relationship you've already built, there's a reasonable chance it'll still be accepted.

But what if the worst happens, and you know your application won't arrive on time, or—even worse—you missed the deadline entirely? First, breathe. Passing out never helped anyone. Second, remember that scholarship providers are human, too. Write to them and ask if you can still submit your application, explaining the reason for the delay if possible (for example, maybe you thought it was a postmark and not arrive-by deadline). Then, offer to do everything possible to get the application to them as soon as possible: e-mail it, overnight it, or both.

It's even better if you've already corresponded with the scholarship provider for some other reason and a relationship has already been built; if so, remind them of that previous correspondence. Explain passionately how you were excited for the scholarship and explain the work you've already done on it (for example, "I have so enjoyed researching Robert Kennedy and couldn't wait to show you what I learned from him about leadership"). Don't lie, obviously, but do demonstrate you are an enthusiastic, quality student who would be an asset to their scholarship program.

Don't think this would work? Think again. Using these techniques, I've been able to submit an application up to a week after the deadline and *still* win the scholarship!

CHAPTER 14:

Final Tips and Tricks

Taxes

Taxes.

Whoohoo, right?

Well, if you're dealing with money, you're going to have to at least understand taxes, and it's not as painful as you may think. Why? Because in the United States much—maybe all—of the "income" you receive through college scholarships will be tax free. With a typical job, you'll lose a great deal of your paycheck to Uncle Sam, but with scholarships, you could get 100% of it. That's awesome. And efficient.

However, your scholarship money is *only* tax free (according to the IRS) if, first, you (or your spouse or dependent) is a degree candidate at an eligible educational institution (most of you reading this will qualify!), and second, if the money is used to pay "qualified education expenses" (tuition and fees required for enrollment/attendance, and sometimes course related books, supplies, and equipment).

If you get enough scholarship money such that all of those qualified education expenses are paid for, any money above and beyond that will be considered taxable income but may still be used for college expenses such as room, board, insurance, student health fees, travel, and any other non-academic or personal expenses (unless the scholarship provider has placed restrictions on its use). Check out **www.irs.gov**, Publication 970, for details and other requirements.

Now, there are two ways in which scholarships may reduce your taxes: first, through "education credits," and second, through a "tuition and fees" deduction. A tax credit is where the government actually reduces the amount of taxes you owe by the amount of the credit. For example, let's say you owe $5,000 in taxes but have a $2,000 tax credit. That means you only have to pay $3,000 in taxes. A tax deduction reduces the amount of income you're paying taxes on so that your taxes are less. For example, let's say your income is $50,000 and your tax deduction is $4,000. That means you'll only be taxed on $46,000 of income, which means you'll pay less taxes.

Okay, now that's out of the way, how does it apply to scholarships? Well, at the time of writing, there were two "education *credits*" available: up to a $2,500 American Opportunity Credit and up to a $2,000 Lifetime Learning Credit. The former is per *student*, the latter is per tax *return*; the former has *more restrictive* qualifications, while the latter *less restrictive*. There are various factors that will affect your qualifications and the amount of money you do or do not get for those credits (such as income limits), so check out IRS form 8863 for details.

There is also up to a $4,000 tax *deduction* per return. Again, there are factors that affect qualifications and amount so be sure to take a look at IRS form 8817. Unfortunately, you can only claim *one* of the credits *or* the deduction for the same student for the same tax year. No stacking!

Even if those credits and deductions are no longer available when you read this, you should still research what tax incentives your government offers and factor that into your college funding strategy. After all, they're there, and they're free. And we're all about free.

Scholarships for Adults

I am often asked if there are scholarships available for adults (i.e., older than traditional college age and returning to school), and the answer is yes! There are essentially two kinds of scholarships adults can apply for:

1. Specific adult scholarships
2. Traditional scholarships without an age limit

For the first point, there are definitely scholarships specifically tailored to adults returning to school, so if you're one of them include words like "adult," "working through college," "returning to college," and "adult education" in your search. The advantage is that there will likely be very few applicants for those scholarships!

For the second point, while many traditional scholarships limit the age of the applicant, some don't. And for those that don't, you can apply! If there's any doubt, of course, contact the scholarship provider, but don't shy away from a scholarship just because it seems geared toward someone younger if there is no specific rule against you applying.

Customizing Your Application

Own that application! You want it to arrive in as good a condition as possible, so don't fold any of the papers—lay them flat in a large manila envelope. Organize the papers logically, with your main application on top and the rest in the order identified on the application. Meaning, if the application you filled out asked for the essay, then the transcript, and then the activities/awards, put them in the envelope in that same order. It just makes it easier for the scholarship provider to keep everything straight.

Next, be meticulous in everything you do and stay detail oriented. For example, here are some things you can do or include to make your application stand out:

> Headers

> Cover pages

> Drop caps

> Color coordination

> Quality, heavy-weight paper

> Calligraphy pens (for signing your name)

> Printed envelopes (versus handwritten)

> Sophisticated typefaces (No Comic Sans. Avoid Comic Sans at all costs.)

> Pictures in the essays (though some applications don't allow that)

In essence, you want to do just about everything your teachers have ever liked in your assignments. You're trying to wow these scholarship providers!

Also, if there is something more you want to include and the application doesn't give you space, *after* carefully checking with the scholarship provider to make sure it's all right, add it in! Just write "See attached sheets" and put in more of what you want—more activities, awards, essays, examples, it's up to you!

Finally, there is nothing worse than having an amazing application that gets lost, separated, or misplaced at the scholarship provider's office. Make sure your name is on every piece of paper (unless it's specified that your essay is being judged "blind" and cannot have your name on it). That way, even if your documents get separated, they'll be able to be pieced back together.

Naming Your Essays

This one little secret will make your mounds of scholarship applications a whole lot easier to keep track of:

Name your essays helpfully.

After three years spent funding college through scholarships, I had literally dozens—if not hundreds—of scholarship essays clogging up my poor computer's hard drive. They were in dozens of folders scattered between "Scholarships 2010" and "Scholarships 2011 summer" and "Scholarships Rejected" and "School and Career," and finding the right one made me feel like I was eight years old again struggling through those interminable *Where's Waldo?* books.

You see, when you're applying for dozens of scholarships, you'll find a lot of overlap, as many scholarships ask for very similar essays. Unless you enjoy broken records and writing like one, it'll save you hours of time if you can just use the same essay repeatedly for different scholarships, merely tweaking it a little to fit the scholarship requirements.

The problem is, you can't do that if you can't find the right scholarship essay. For example, don't name them the following:

1. kind of long essay for pteradactyl scholarship version 9.32
2. scholarship essay short
3. Version 6 Scholarship Application Essay, May 6, 2012, for Future Mosquito Conservationists of America United, Due May 19, 2012, Complete

These are not helpful.

Instead, organize all your scholarship essays in electronic folders by year (a year from now, you'll write new essays as your plans will need to be updated). Then name them similar to the following template: [Word Count] [Subject] Scholarship Essay for [Provider], Version [X]

For example, I might name my essay I'm working on, "500 word life goals scholarship essay for FFA, version 6." That way, a month from now, when I need another 500-word life goals essay, I'll have one ready to go. Even if I need a 1,000-word or 200-word life goals essay, I'll have my 500-word essay as a convenient template.

Naming essays this way will streamline your application process, because after all, scholarships should be about serving you, not consuming you.

Communication

Here is Joe. Joe is a very nice young man who wrote a lovely scholarship essay. He was involved in volunteer work with his school, plays basketball all the time, and likes fluffy little puppies. He is a fabulous candidate for Awesome Astronauts Anonymous Scholarship.

Here is Sally. Sally is a very nice young woman who also wrote a lovely scholarship essay, travels around her state speaking about the dangers of drunk driving, and likes Chipotle and living green. She is also a wonderful candidate for the scholarship.

So who gets it?

Well, what if I told you Joe had e-mailed Mary, the scholarship coordinator, three weeks ago asking if he could include extra sheets about his activities and awards (and he said "please" and "thank you" to boot). And then, when he sent off his application, he sent Mary another e-mail stating how much he enjoyed writing the essay about awesome anonymous astronauts and how he wished her all the best in choosing a qualified candidate for her scholarship.

Joe will have a better chance of getting that scholarship. Not because he's way better than Sally, but because Mary has to make a decision on who wins the scholarship *somehow*. And why not—if the applications themselves are basically equal—choose the student who is most motivated, respectful, communicative, and passionate about the scholarship?

Even more, Joe would be in a much better situation if he had a problem with his application (such as it getting lost in the mail), because Mary may be inclined to give him the benefit of the doubt that he really is conscientious, and after all, it's not really his fault the post office lost his application.

The moral of the story? Communicate with the scholarship provider. If you have a question, ask it. If you have a comment (as long as it's polite), say it. If you are thankful for the opportunity, tell them. Don't be shy, because people who don't communicate don't easily fund college through scholarships.

When You've Won

Believe it or not, winning a scholarship isn't the end. After you win one, there are a few things you need to remember.

First, write a thank-you note—handwritten on quality stationery—as soon as you hear you've won. The salutation of the note should be specific—make it out to highest person in the company (ex., the executive), the person in charge of the scholarship itself, and then the company as a whole (ex., "Dear Mr. John Smith, Ms. Sally Peterson, and Dandelion Growers United"). However, it's usually best to physically mail that thank-you note to whomever you sent your original application to, versus the executive or the general contact address for the business. That way you'll be sure to get it to the right person.

Second, if there is an awards ceremony the scholarship provider wants you to attend, make every effort to go. Even if you didn't win the scholarship but were a runner-up and they invite you, go! Not only is it common courtesy, but winning scholarships is all about building relationships. Going to an awards ceremony will help you build relationships, network for your future career, and, if the scholarship is one you can apply for year after year, may help you get the scholarship next time because of the deepened contacts you have with the people there. Be sure to write a second thank-you note after the awards ceremony as well to thank them for their hospitality and recognition of your achievement.

Finally, find out if you can apply for the scholarship again next year. This is because there are three main types of scholarships:

1. Scholarships you can win once
2. Scholarships you can win multiple times but have to apply for every year

3. Scholarships that are automatically renewed (ex., winning it once will give you $4,000 a year for four years)

If the scholarship is automatically renewed, make sure you know how to keep it that way: do you have to provide them a transcript each semester? Do you need to submit a short, basic re-application?

If the scholarship is not automatically renewed but you can apply for it again, learn what they liked about your last scholarship, and, of course, re-apply. If the scholarship providers don't give you any feedback in the award letter or awards ceremony, you can always write them and ask for it! They'll be impressed you want to improve as a writer and student.

If you can't re-apply, that's fine. Someone else will be aided by the scholarship, and you can move on to others!

CHAPTER 15:

Other Ways to Fund College

As I said earlier, you should plan to fund 100% of college through scholarships. However, there's nothing wrong with saving money to make that process easier, and there are many amazing books and resources out there on that subject. I'll just touch on them here so you can have an idea of where else to look to help fund your college adventure.

Saving Money

Which college education would be easier to fund through scholarships: a $100,000 one or a $10,000 one? Well, that's a simple answer. But, surprisingly, it's an answer that is often overlooked. Meaning, be sure you have minimized your college expenses before trying to fund college through scholarships. Here are some ways to do that:

1. **Take high school Advanced Placement (AP) classes**. Taking AP classes in high school can often count toward your college education, reducing the number of classes you have to take in college, thereby reducing the time you spend there and the amount of money you have to pay.

2. **Pass CLEP tests**. The College Level Examination Program (CLEP) tests cover subjects from management to American history, and taking and passing one of these 90-minute exams generally counts as passing its semester-long (but sometimes one- or two-year long) college course equivalent. They're pretty hard tests, and you'll need to study for them with a study guide, but that's still cheaper and faster than taking the entire course. Go to **www.clep.collegeboard.org** for more details.

3. **Utilize PSEO**. Some states offer Post-Secondary Education Options (PSEO), where as a high school student you can take college classes, either in person or through distance education. Taking them is free and usually gives "dual credit"—meaning, taking a PSEO class in history might satisfy your high school history requirement for that semester as well as counting toward your college degree. Just be careful—not all PSEO credits from one college transfer cleanly to the college you end up attending. So if you already know what college you want to attend after high school, check them out first to see what will and won't transfer.

4. **Fill out your FAFSA**. The Free Application for Federal Student Aid (FAFSA) helps you get government money (such as grants and loans) and assists your college in providing financial aid. Most colleges require you to fill this out. Do it.

5. **Take summer school and/or distance education courses**. Summer school can often help you save money, particularly if you take the classes online or live at home while doing them. Distance education courses can save you even more—if you can't afford to go to a school in person, you can always take a semester (or more) of distance education courses. Some students take all their generals distance ed through a very inexpensive online school, transfer those credits to their "main" school, and take all their specialized courses in person at their main school. Distance ed courses are

nice because you can do them on your own time and so potentially work (or apply for scholarships!) more easily.

6. **Your employer's tuition reimbursement.** Check out your employer to see if they offer any credits, tuition reimbursement, or other financial aid in your quest. Even if they don't, if you can make a legitimate case why your higher education will benefit the company, try crafting a proposal requesting aid and submitting it. In essence what you're doing is pursuing an unadvertised scholarship (talk about a small applicant pool!). The worst they can say is no. And if they say yes, then in addition to the financial assistance you may also help set a precedent to assist your co-workers with their higher education goals. Everyone wins.

7. **Utilize military and other specific aid.** If you're in or were in the military, the Post 9/11 G.I. Bill can provide significant tuition aid, but there are some regulations, so check out the Department of Veterans Affairs (http://www.va.gov/) for up-to-date information. Also, minorities and single parents, particularly single mothers, also will often get specific grad school scholarships, so be sure to include those keywords in your search for best results.

These are all great ways to reduce overall college expenses so you have less to pay through scholarships.

Making Money

Is there ever a time when it is better not to try to fund college 100% through scholarships? There may be a few situations where this is the case:

1. **You aren't taking a full load.** If your load per semester is fewer than 12 credits, you won't qualify for most scholarships, as generally they require you to have full-time college status.

2. **For some reason, you simply aren't getting scholarships**.

Perhaps you deeply struggle with writing, simply cannot figure out what you want to do with your life, can't find the motivation, or, despite everything, simply are not getting scholarships. In this situation, look for on-campus jobs to minimize commute time, take full advantage of every way you can to save money for college (as described above), or even find a less expensive school. Don't give up your dreams of college—but at the same time, don't let college force you to give up your dreams because of too much debt.

However, please don't give up on scholarships. Keep looking, learn from your challenges and mistakes, and apply, apply, apply. Even the best actors rarely get booked more than once every 20 or more auditions—and it's no different for scholarships.

CHAPTER 16:

A Little Humor (because you made it to the end!)

I Apologize for Your Many Problems

I hate to break it to you, but you might have some more problems in your life now that you're funding college through scholarships, as scholarships are awesome right up until they aren't. Here are the top ten problems you might have if you fund college through scholarships:

1. You never go more than a few weeks without braving the depths of the tunnels and catacombs of your college to enter the financial aid office to drop off a check (fighting off all the zombies who were trapped down there a decade ago).

2. You thought you were done writing thank you notes after your high school graduation open house? Ha. Haha.

3. You have so many bookmarked tabs from hours of Internet scholarship Googling that you consider dedicating a separate browser entirely to your scholarship search.

4. People assume you're on Facebook all those hours you're spending on the Internet and get mad that you're not accepting their little FarmVille requests.

5. You forget what spring breaks are. What? Break? What is this of which you speak? Haven't I been applying for scholarships every break since elementary school?

6. When people ask your life goals, you freak them out by instantly spouting off a 1,000-word polished speech outlining exactly what you're doing, why, and how, ending it dramatically with a persuasive appeal on why they should give you money to support you in that endeavor.

7. Your financial aid counselor is ready to ban you from the school for how many times she's had to decrease the amount of loans you get. You're actually kind of afraid to make eye contact with her in the hall in case she thinks you're about to make another appointment.

8. You no longer have a good reason to not go to grad school or get a double or triple major because you know you could stay in school for as long as you want.

9. You can rattle off the definitions of subsidized loan, unsubsidized loan, Stafford loan, expected family contribution, and tuition subsidies in your sleep even though you still can't remember your best friend's phone number. This makes your best friend annoyed.

10. You are spoiled forever for "real" jobs because they're not giving you $1,000 per hour.

So, I'm sorry if funding college through scholarships causes issues for you. I hope you'll manage. It's worth it, after all.

Cool Things You Can Do With the Money You Saved

I don't know how much your dream school costs. Maybe $10,000 per year. Maybe $100,000. Regardless, what could you do with all that money you're not spending on school because you're funding college through scholarships?

1. $20,000 (a $5,000/year school) = 40,000 Krispy Kreme doughnuts (and a super-sized stomach ache)

2. $40,000 (a $10,000/year school) = $1,256,376.80 if you invest it at 9% annual compound interest for the next 40 years until you retire (not only did you fund scholarships through college, you became a millionaire because of it!)

3. $60,000 (a $15,000/year school) = 0.92 nights in the Royal Penthouse Suites in Geneva, Switzerland (What's 0.92 nights? I don't know. It's kind of like having 2.4 kids.)

4. $120,000 (a $30,000/year school) = a nice little uninhabited island in Fiji (in case you went to college to be a hermit)

5. $200,000 (a $50,000/year school) = 5 minutes in space aboard Virgin Galactic (do you realize that's $667 per second?)

Okay, so even if you don't do any of those things, you have to admit— it'll be nice to have the extra cash you'll get from funding college through scholarships.

Top 10 Most Bizarre College Scholarships

You think there are no scholarships out there for you.
Ha.

Be prepared to have your mind blown. Here are the top 10 weirdest scholarships I've found, and they're proof there are scholarships out there for even the most out-of-the-box person ever.

1. **Tall people** (Tall Clubs International)

Are you a girl and above 5'10"? A guy taller than 6'3"? There you go.

2. **Short people (Little People of America)**

Not tall? Super short? Don't worry, just apply for this scholarship.

3. **Left handers** (Juanita College)

You can finally get some payback (literally) for always getting pencil smudged on your hand when you write. And considering only about 10% of the world's population is left handed, you have a pretty good chance at this scholarship, provided you attend Juanita College.

4. **Vacuum coaters** (Society of Vacuum Coaters Foundation)

If you like to vacuum coat, this is your chance. If you're like me and have not the faintest idea what vacuum coating is (fashion design for vacuum cleaners?), then maybe skip this one.

5. **People who know stuff but not specific stuff** (Common Knowledge Scholarship Foundation)

Stop complaining you have no specific skills. You have the specific skill of having no specific skills. Get money with it.

6. **Klingon speakers** (Klingon Language Institute)

No kidding. See it to believe it. *romuluSngan Hol yIjatlh. He'So' QIchIIj.*

7. **Members of Starfleet** (The International Star Trek Fan Association, Inc.)

This just keeps getting better and better.

8. **Participants in a nudist colony** (American Nudist Research Library)

I think I'd rather be a part of Starfleet.

9. **Bagpipe majors** (Carnegie Mellon University)

Considering only Carnegie Mellon University offers a major in bagpipes, if you qualify for this, you *really* qualify.

10. People who sound like ducks (Stuttgart)

Well, *there's* a skill that's finally come in handy, huh?

There are a lot more weird scholarships out there, too, so get out there, find a couple, and start funding college through them!

CHAPTER 17:

Summary

The 15 Main Points

Completely overwhelmed yet? Don't worry, this chapter is a culmination of everything you truly need to know. So what are the main points we covered?

1. Don't hate scholarships. Doing them right is efficient, fun, and the best paying job you'll ever have.

2. Have a mindset that, "Scholarships will pay for college." Don't give yourself an out.

3. Remember the time commitment is like a job, not extracurricular.

4. Know *why* what you want to do (or think you may want to do, or would love to do) is your heart passion and is going to change the world.

5. Keep all your scholarships organized in a master Excel workbook.

6. Find your scholarships on search engines, Google, and other sources

7. The key to getting scholarships is finding the ones you are (1) very qualified for and (2) no one else knows about.

8. Choose scholarships for which you are fabulously qualified, not merely technically qualified.

9. Remember the ten rules for writing scholarship essays.

10. Find and keep great references.

11. Have a lot of transcripts ready.

12. Know that all of these tips apply to grad school.

13. Know your deadlines and meet them.

14. Take advantage of tax credits and deductions, know how adult scholarships work, customize your application, name your essays well, have good communication, and be a gracious winner.

15. Minimize college expenses as much as possible.

The many other little tips I've mentioned throughout the book will help, but they are icing on the cake compared to these 15 main points.

Timeline

These charts lay out exactly what you need to do and when.

General Timeline	
Time	**Description**
Early as possible	Track honors/activities/awards
Minimum 8th grade	Start scholarship search
Minimum 9th grade	Start applying for scholarships
Getting started	Put together Excel workbook with necessary pages
Monthly	Look for scholarships online
Each semester	Request updated transcripts
Yearly	Update Excel workbook and references

Individual Application Timeline	
Time Before Deadline	**Description**
6 weeks	Determine necessary materials
5 weeks	Send out reference letter requests
4 weeks	Write essays and compile documents (ex., honors/awards)
3 weeks	Collect reference letters
3 weeks	Edit and compile all documents
2 weeks	Mail application
3 days	Follow up application with e-mail

Checklist

Gather these together before you start on your scholarship adventure.

1. Excel workbook
2. Reference list
3. Expenses sheet
4. Zinch profile
5. FastWeb profile
6. Scholarships.com profile
7. Hobbies and interests list
8. A pet dragon
9. Supportive friend(s)
10. Understanding of life passions/dreams
11. Transcripts (high school and college, if applicable)
12. Activities/awards spreadsheet
13. Four basic scholarship essays
14. Person to edit your essays

Database

I admit it. I had this crippling fear that somehow, somewhere, there was some scholarship search engine that had every single scholarship I was qualified for, and I would miss out on tens of thousands of dollars just because I missed that one single Holy Grail search engine. Driven by this fear, I checked out over 20 different search engines, and I found that, while going to multiple engines was helpful, in the end, none was the magic bullet. But in case you're interested, here's what I found (evaluated, of course, at the time of writing):

Military.com/education	Good, specific to military.
CareersandColleges	Not helpful.
CollegeBoard	Easy form and good results.
CollegeData	Decent, some good scholarships.
CollegeNet	Hundreds, but mostly specific to a college.
ECampusTours	Hard to use and not worth it.
FastAp.org	Not helpful.
FastWeb	Good.
FindTuition	Not helpful.
Free4U	Had a form too long to fill out.
FreschInfo	Not helpful.
MyCollegeOptions	Good.
MyFreeDegree	Hard to use and not worth it.
Scholarships101	Not helpful.
ScholarshipMonkey	Not helpful.
Scholarship-Page	Not helpful.
ScholarshipExperts	Some, but not a lot.
Scholarships.com	Very good, lots of unique scholarships.
ScholarSite	Not helpful.
SchoolSoup	Hundreds, but mostly specific to a college.
StudentScholarshipSearch	Not helpful.
SuperCollege	Not helpful.
Zinch	Wonderful! They double your scholarships

CHAPTER 18:

Who on Earth Are You? And Other FAQs

A brown-haired girl with braids raised her hand for the sixth time in the question-and-answer period after one of my talks on scholarship.

"Okay, last question, I promise. But I have to know—how many scholarships have you won?"

People are always fascinated by hearing my story and have many questions about me and about scholarships in general. Here are a few.

1. How many scholarships have you won?

I won about thirty scholarships over the course of three years, totaling approximately $100,000. This paid for my tuition, room and board, books, and a study trip to Israel after graduation. Best paying job I'll ever have!

2. What was your success rate in winning scholarships?

It's hard to tell, because I only developed a better system for keeping track of my scholarships later on. Also, the more years I applied, the better my success rate became, because I started applying smarter, not harder. But I estimate that I won approximately 25% of the scholarships for which I applied.

3. What is your GPA?

Don't freak out. Grades aren't everything. Having said that, I was a 4.00 GPA in college with an interdisciplinary major that took me through classes from public relations to accounting to ministry to theatre. But remember, grades aren't what get you scholarships. *You* are what gets you scholarships.

4. How are you so *motivated*?

I consider this one of the funniest questions of all, because actually, I don't always consider myself that motivated, at least, not regarding scholarship hunting; it was just so logical I didn't need to dredge up much extra motivation. Honestly, I consider the students who work 20 or more hours per week while taking a full load of classes the incredibly motivated ones. Hats off to those students—they're the ones that deserve your respect for motivation. Instead, I just had to figure out how to spend a few hours a week getting scholarships.

5. What are you doing now?

Well, I briefly considered making applying for scholarships my full-time job for the next 40 years, but then I decided I needed a life. Therefore, I have delved into my other passions—writing books like this (www.thousanddollarhour.com), horse training (www.cambriahorsemanship.com), acting and modeling (www.hannahrivard.com), and writing (www.prayersoflight.blogspot.com).

However, what I always sought to bring out in my scholarship essays are my greatest passions. And without a doubt, what fills me with the most joy and reveals to me the greatest beauty is my King, Jesus Christ. He has created a kingdom here on earth of wonder beyond our wildest dreams, and the greatest adventure of all is living in His glory.

CHAPTER 19:

Have at It!

At the beginning of this book, I promised that by the end you'd know a few secrets. In case you didn't catch them, let's recap:

1. **The number one place people should be looking for cholarships—and never do.**

Answer: It starts with a G.

2. **How to double your money on select scholarships with a single mouse click.**

Answer: It starts with a Z.

3. **The way to exponentially increase your chances of getting a scholarship simply by the process of elimination.**

Answer: Use the three-question approach of "Am I qualified?"

4. **The piece of the scholarship timeline that no one I've ever met has done, but can get you tons of money.**

Answer: If you're past 8th grade (really, if you're older than age 5), you're already behind.

5. **The scholarship search engine everyone uses but is one you could practically forget about.**

Answer: It's the opposite of a slow web.

6. How you know what scholarships you'll probably never get so you can save time and forget about them.

Answer: It relates to how good a story you can tell.

Even if you didn't remember the answers to those questions, that's okay. The most important parts to remember are passion, freedom, and dedication: the *passion* for your dreams and your vision for the world; the *freedom* from debt and from the constraints of low-paying jobs or colleges you don't want to attend; and the *dedication* to live in that passion and freedom through funding college through scholarships.

That sort of life is out there for you. The choice is yours as to whether you will claim it.

IF YOU HAVE QUESTIONS:
Support and Speaking

You may still have questions after this book, and I don't blame you—scholarships can be overwhelming! Please feel free to contact me through any of the following ways, and I'd love to help you out:

1. **Facebook** (**www.facebook.com/thousanddollarhour**)
2. **Twitter** (**https://twitter.com/1000DollarHour**)
3. **E-mail** (**info@thousanddollarhour.com**)
4. **Website/Blog** (**www.thousanddollarhour.com**)

I also do individual scholarship coaching, where I not only provide personal consultation through Skype or e-mail, but I can find scholarships for you, edit your scholarship essays, review your applications, and much more! Just check out my website for the current rates and how to get started.

Similarly, let me know if you have success stories coming from tips you learned in this book! I'd love to feature you on my blog or even in my next book.

And as hopefully is obvious by this book, I love writing, but I also love speaking. I have spoken to many people and groups about finding scholarships, including honors programs, college funding organizations, and college preview days. I'm as comfortable speaking to a room of two hundred people as I am meeting small groups for coffee.

There are many groups I enjoy speaking to, including 4-H and FFA clubs, youth groups, college preview days, current college students, high schools and junior highs, scholarship providers, college funding organizations, community education programs, and teachers and principals.

I can speak on any of the following topics or develop a custom talk tailored to your group's needs:

1. **Finding and winning scholarships**
2. **Writing the perfect scholarship essay**
3. **How to develop your life goals so college and scholarships work to fulfill them**
4. **How I kept a 4.00 GPA in college**
5. **Keeping an education-life balance while in college**
6. **The top ten scholarship myths**

I would love to come speak to your group, no matter where you're located (I love traveling)! Please contact me to set up your customized talk!

thou$and
h🕐ur dollar ™